ALSO BY DR. BOB ROTELLA

Books

Golf Is Not a Game of Perfect
Golf Is a Game of Confidence
The Golf of Your Dreams
Parenting Your Superstar

Audio Tapes

Playing to Win—Golf, Business, Life
Golfing Out of Your Mind
Putting Out of Your Mind
Focusing Your Mind for Competition

Videotape

Putt to Win (with Brad Faxon)

LIFE IS NOT
A GAME OF PERFECT

Finding Your Real Talent and
Making It Work for You

DR. BOB ROTELLA

WITH BOB CULLEN

Simon & Schuster

SIMON & SCHUSTER
Rockefeller Center
1230 Avenue of the Americas
New York, NY 10020

Simon & Schuster and colophon are registered trademarks
of Simon & Schuster Inc.

Designed by Jeanette Olender
Manufactured in the United States of America

1   3   5   7   9   10   8   6   4   2

Library of Congress Cataloging-in-Publication Data
Rotella, Robert J.
Life is not a game of perfect: finding your real talent and
making it work for you/Bob Rotella with Bob Cullen
p. cm.
1. Success—Psychological aspects. 2. Personality.
3. Attitude (Psychology). I. Cullen, Bob. II. Title.
BF637.S8R624   1999
158.1—dc21   98-54819   CIP
ISBN 0-684-84286-6

To my mom and dad and aunts and uncles,
for all they taught us; and to my daughter, Casey,
for what she continues to teach me

CONTENTS

—

INTRODUCTION

I'm a sports psychologist. My specialty is teaching golfers, tennis players, basketball players, and other athletes how to enhance their performance by thinking in the most effective way possible. I help them make their minds as skilled and powerful as their bodies.

So what am I doing writing a book about performance enhancement outside the sporting arena?

It's a fair question.

Fifteen years ago, I might not have attempted this book. I was focused strictly on sport, on the ways that the minds of great athletes operated.

But over the past fifteen years, the scope of my work has gradually expanded. Companies like General Electric and Merrill Lynch have asked me to work with their people on enhancing performance in the workplace. I speak to their employees and managers. Some come to me for personal counseling. Over time, I've gotten to know some of them very well. And among the amateur golfers I work with I've begun to see a growing number of people with great life and career achievements, people determined to become as good at golf as they are in business. Their stories and experiences have all en-lightened me.

I've come to understand that a sport like golf has a great deal in common with a competitive business. I've learned that many of the same character traits possessed by champion ath-letes are critical to the success of people in any endeavor.

I've also noticed that despite the almost obsessive attention our society pays to sports, the media generally obfuscate, rather than illuminate, the real factors behind the success of the heroes we lionize. We marvel at the play of a Michael Jor-dan, but we don't learn the appropriate lessons about what makes Michael Jordan the player he is.

Thus, this book. It's about what I call real talent—the traits and attitudes that help people achieve greatness. It's a book of good news, because I believe that every human being is born with the most fundamental of real talents—free will. I believe that anyone, if he or she chooses to apply free will to the de-velopment of the traits and attitudes I'll describe, can succeed.

LIFE IS NOT A GAME OF PERFECT

CHAPTER ONE

Brilliance of a Different Sort

Most of us think we know what talent is.

We hear a soprano hit and hold a clear, high C and we think she's talented. We see a basketball player soar above the defense, turn in the air, and jam the ball through the hoop for two points. We think he's talented. We see a skinny kid in the front row of a math class who effortlessly glides through calculus and scores an 800 on the SAT test. We think he's talented.

Talent, we think, is something granted or withheld by fate. It's in our genes or it's not in our genes. It's speed and leaping ability. It's a lyrical voice. It's a facile mastery of calculus. And we think that talent, defined in this way, by and large determines an individual's ability to succeed.

Television and the press reinforce this notion. They glorify the precocious, natural achievers and make it seem as if they live on a mountaintop high above the valley in which the rest of the world plods along.

I don't dispute that the soprano, the math whiz, and the slam-dunk artist have talent as talent is conventionally defined.

But in twenty-five years as a psychologist, working with people who want to succeed in fields ranging from golf to finance, I've learned that this conventional talent, while important and helpful, is not sufficient to make an individual successful. In many cases, it's not even necessary. I've learned that other abilities and qualities, traits of character less easily observed than physical gifts or test scores, do lead to success. These traits are brilliance of a different sort. They comprise what I call real talent.

This book is about real talent. It's a book of good news, because unlike the talent to hit high C or execute the tomahawk slam, real talent doesn't depend on your genes. *Real talent is something anyone can develop.*

⋆⟶

Take the case of a friend of mine, Bob Sherman. Bob grew up in the 1950s in Durand, Michigan, a small town near Lansing and Flint. He was the quintessential small-town sports star. He quarterbacked the football team. He ran the hurdles on the track team. He excelled in baseball. In fact, he attracted a bonus offer from the Boston Red Sox organization. In an athletic sense, he seemed well endowed with conventional talent.

But his parents had not been to able to go to college, and they were determined that Bob would. "They saw a college degree as a way of getting out of the blue-collar world, of getting a high-class job," Bob recalls.

So he turned down the Red Sox, temporarily, and chose to go to the University of Iowa on a football scholarship. Iowa, unlike some of the other schools that recruited him, did not insist that he forgo baseball in favor of spring football practice. But Iowa was, in those days, a football powerhouse, and an interesting thing happened to Bob when he got there. He found out that he was no longer considered supremely talented in the conventional sense of the word.

He was still as fast and as agile as he had been at home in Durand. But there were faster, more agile athletes at Iowa. And a lot of them were bigger than Bob was. In the context of big-time college athletics, Bob recalls, "I wasn't very gifted. I didn't have great ability."

He had to adjust. He didn't lose faith in his physical gifts. He still believed in them. But he understood that they were no longer sufficient. If he was going to succeed at Iowa, he had to discover his real talent.

And he did. He started with some of the qualities of character his parents had instilled in him. They had always told him the important thing was doing his best. They had helped him to learn that there is no shame in failure if you fail after giving everything you have. "I decided," Bob remembers, "that I might get beat out, but no one would outwork me."

So he threw himself into football competition. His coaches suggested that if he wanted to play, he would have to give up being a quarterback and learn to play defense. He did that. He spent a lot of time on the bench, but he became a starter at halfback in his senior year. He wasn't a star for Iowa, but he was a very solid player. And he ran the hurdles and played baseball for the Hawkeyes, still planning a professional baseball career.

More important, the attitude he had to develop to keep playing football manifested itself in his studies. Bob was determined to get his degree before his football scholarship ran out. Not many star athletes at Iowa felt that way. They fell prey to the notion that floats about in our society that talent determines everything. They had lots of fans and coaches telling them how talented they were, so they felt no need for discipline or hard work in their studies. Bob Sherman, on the other hand, perceived himself as someone with limited gifts who would have to work hard to get what he wanted. And he did. He majored in biological science with a psychology minor, thinking that he might coach when he finished school and professional baseball. He had to manage his time very carefully to compete in three sports and keep his grades up. In his fraternity, among his peers, he developed a reputation as a bit of a grind. Some people teased him because he was always either practicing or studying. He ignored them.

In the spring of his senior year at Iowa, two things happened. First, Bob was drafted, in the twelfth round, by the

Pittsburgh Steelers. He put away the letter informing him of his selection, thinking that it might someday make an interesting souvenir. He had no intention of playing professional football, at least not until the second thing happened. Bob was with the Iowa baseball team on a road trip in Arizona when he tore the rotator cuff in his throwing arm. This was before the days of either microscopic surgery or the designated hitter. If you tore your rotator cuff you couldn't throw, and if you couldn't throw there was no place for you in baseball. Bob's path to the big leagues was blocked.

He took another look at the Steelers' offer. A twelfth-round draft pick was not exactly a hot commodity. In fact, the National Football League has since trimmed its draft to fewer than twelve rounds. A twelfth-round pick was not expected to start, or even to make the team. A twelfth-round pick was either a project—someone the scouts thought had potential that had not been developed in college—or he was fodder for the taxi squad, someone for the real players to hit during practice.

But Bob, by this time, was used to being perceived as less than supremely talented, and he was beginning to perceive that talent wasn't necessarily what the scouts thought it was. He accepted a bonus from the Steelers in the $2,000 range and reported to camp. He made the team as a defensive back.

For two more years, Bob threw himself into football. He became a starter for the Steelers. But at the professional level, his body simply wasn't big enough or durable enough. He remembers one time being knocked cold by Hall of Fame receiver Charley Taylor of the Redskins. He remembers playing with hamstring muscles that were black-and-blue from the tearing and pounding they got. It seemed that every time he was about to establish himself in the Steelers' defensive backfield, he got hurt. In 1966, the Steelers let him go in the expansion draft that stocked the Atlanta Falcons. Bob hurt his hamstring again. The Falcons cut him.

Bob decided he had had enough of football. His physical talent had taken him as far as it could. It was time to see where his real talent could take him.

He had developed an interest in stocks and bonds. He liked the financial markets. He also liked the fact that people who worked in them generally derived their income from commissions. In pro football, his income had been limited to his contractual salary. No matter how hard he worked, no matter how successful he was, the contract determined what he would be paid. In the financial world, there was no ceiling on compensation. He wouldn't have to worry about persuading some coach to give him playing time. He wouldn't have to worry about the quality of his team. He and his attitude controlled his destiny. That's true of many jobs in the adult world, and it's one of the reasons people with real talent often blossom in adulthood. They love the opportunity to answer to no one but themselves, to set their own standards and meet them.

Bob wanted to work for Merrill Lynch, then as now the

biggest brokerage firm on Wall Street. He didn't have the right contacts. He couldn't get in. He worked for another company for a year, and then he reapplied to Merrill Lynch. This time he was accepted. He started in Merrill Lynch's Detroit office in 1967.

Starting as a financial consultant without a lot of rich friends wasn't easy. Bob culled newspapers, magazines, anything he could find to generate lists of prospects, people who might have some money to invest. Then he called on them. He worked three or four nights per week and most Saturdays. He drove wherever he had to drive to meet with someone willing to listen to his presentation on stocks and mutual funds.

His failure rate was high but not atypical. In his early days, perhaps one call in twenty-five generated a sale.

What separated Bob from most of the beginning brokers was his attitude, which was part of his real talent. He didn't see himself as a natural salesman, but he knew the value of perseverance. He would persevere when others would not. He would devote himself to thinking of ways to succeed rather than thinking of things that rationalized failure.

As a result of that attitude, he never felt sorry for himself when a prospect said no. He chose to see such calls as small successes. "It was knocking a bad prospect off my list. That brought me one step closer to the good prospect," he recalls.

The difference between successful and unsuccessful salespeople, he found, is that "most people will starve before they'll put themselves in a position to be told no. To succeed in this business, you have to have the courage to put yourself in a position where you can fail."

As we'll see, that attitude about failure is one of the characteristics of real talent.

Bob rose in the company and today he is in charge of Merrill Lynch's operations in the eastern region of the United States. That's where I've come to know him, because I frequently consult with Merrill Lynch's management on ways to find and develop the kind of talent Bob displayed as a young broker—real talent.

It's not easy, because real talent is difficult to measure. While you have to be reasonably intelligent to be a successful financial consultant, Bob has found that college grades and IQ scores are not a good predictor of success. "The world is full of 4.0s who can't succeed in business," he says.

Interestingly, he's also found that success in athletics is also a poor predictor. The reason, he believes, is that the best athletes get the wrong message about talent. "A lot of them had so much physical ability that success in athletics came easily for them. They think it should happen easily in the business world, too. They think the world owes them a living," Bob explains. "The athletes who succeed in business are generally not the ones who were stars on the field. They're the linebackers who were too small and had to work hard just to get on the team. They transfer that ability to make commitments and sacrifices to the business world, and they do well."

But there aren't enough feisty little linebackers knocking on the door at Merrill Lynch or any other company. Bob has found that the best candidates are people who have shown themselves successful in other tasks that require real talent. That reduces the pool pretty quickly. In comparison to ex-jocks and people with perfect scores on the SAT, people with real talent are hard to find.

It used to be, Bob tells me, that only one in five of Merrill Lynch's new hires worked out. The other four, within a few years, had left, either voluntarily or involuntarily. They couldn't meet the sales figures that Merrill Lynch expects of its financial consultants.

In the past few years, after paying great attention to screening and training, Merrill Lynch has improved its ratio of successful new financial consultants to one in four. That seems like a low batting average, but in the world in which Merrill Lynch operates, the world of sophisticated sales, it's quite respectable.

When I speak to new financial consultants at Merrill Lynch, I start out by telling them that I'm blown away by the dimensions of the opportunity that's been laid before them. They're going to work for the Chicago Bulls of their business. The best available research, analysis, and client services are at their disposal. Their company's name alone is going to open doors for them. There is no limit to the amount of money they can earn. Even better, they have the opportunity to do some good in the world by providing clients with financial security.

Just ask the people who bought mutual funds from Bob Sherman in the 1960s how well they've done over the past thirty years.

And yet, three in four will fail to take advantage of that opportunity.

I think that's a reflection of the way our society raises children. Our schools and our families devote enormous attention to cultivating the personal characteristics that we have been told comprise talent. American parents spend lavishly on private schools and tutors and prep courses to improve their children's scores on an endless series of acronymic intelligence tests, from the first IQ to the last GRE. After school and in the summer they devote copious resources to the things that television tells us are the athletic talents—dunking or dribbling or driving golf balls.

But I know of few if any school programs that teach and develop the characteristics of real talent. If the typical school pays any attention at all to personal strength of character, it wastes its time on superficial efforts to assure that each child has high self-esteem. Regardless of how the children perform, it tells them that they're great, they're marvelous, they're talented. Kids see through this. It does no good.

In the end, our system spews out millions of graduates who become the three out of four who fail to grasp the opportunity they're afforded by companies like Merrill Lynch. Because ours is a wealthy society, they don't starve. For the most part, they find niches where mediocrity is tolerated. They go on to have careers of no particular distinction. They retire with a vague sense of dissatisfaction and bitterness. They keep the psychiatrists and the makers of Prozac in business.

I see this as a terrible loss. I know that this society could be unimaginably more productive and a great deal happier if people knew the truth about talent and acted on it.

And I see myself as very fortunate, because I grew up in a home and in a town and at a time in which real talent was appreciated and cultivated.

CHAPTER TWO

What I Learned in Rutland

`I've recently been working with a newcomer to the LPGA Tour, Stefania Croce from Italy. She's got one of the best golf swings I've ever seen, and she's a cheerful, optimistic player with a big smile. I think she's going to do very well over here.

Stefania told me something that started me thinking about my roots. On my father's side, my ancestors are Sicilian. Stefania knows the territory and knows the people. Sicilians have endured some hard times. For centuries, they were subjugated and exploited by northern Italians. They had to scratch for opportunity. They had to suffer through oppression. Sometimes the process of subjugation, while inexcusable, can have a positive side effect. It tends to winnow out those without the strength of character to endure it. Stefania says that, whatever the reason, the people who come from my ancestral lands in Sicily are known for persistence. That's not to say that all Sicilians are persistent or that only Sicilians are persistent. I've met people from dozens of different cultures who have developed this trait. It just may be a little more prevalent among Sicilians. As Stefania says, they don't give up.

That certainly describes my grandparents and my parents, all of whom taught me a lot about real talent. My paternal grandfather came to America from Sicily in the early years of this century and, like many other Italians, found work in the stone business. In 1927, he was promoted to a position as yard foreman at the Rutland Marble Finishing Co. in Rutland, Vermont. Shortly thereafter, he was killed when a marble block fell off a crane in the yard and crushed him. My Dad, at this time, was eight years old.

My grandmother was left with eight children to raise, but she was not without resources—the resources of character she brought over from Sicily. Without complaining, she made do. She took in boarders. She and her daughters took in sewing, finishing belts from a Rutland garment factory every night after dinner. They had a chicken coop and a garden.

Of course, they had help from the community. Each spring, men who had emigrated from my grandfather's village in Sicily would come by with a plow and a horse to break ground for the garden. Each autumn they would drop off a load of firewood to help the Rotellas through the winter. And one member of the community, a barber, suggested that my grandmother send my father to his shop to help out and learn a trade. She did. He worked in the shop from the time he was nine years old.

Depression and war prevented my father from getting as much formal education as he wanted. When he graduated from Mt. St. Joseph's Academy in Rutland, there was no money for college. So he bought a barbershop and worked it for two years until he had saved enough to pay the tuition—then about thirty dollars a semester—at the University of Alabama. But before he could complete his studies, World War II broke out. He joined the Navy and in the Navy he met my mother, Laura. They married and started a family that would eventually grow to five children. Dad went back into barbering to support us.

But I never heard him complain about the luck he'd had. Instead, he served as my first role model.

In his business, he taught me to appreciate customers. He would never let a customer walk out of the shop unless he looked exactly right. He would never turn away a customer who knocked on the door five minutes after closing time. When a customer was sick, Dad made it a practice to visit the man in the hospital and give him a free trim.

He knew that it was their business that allowed him to take care of his family. He knew that he didn't deserve their business by divine right. He had to earn it. He was grateful that their patronage freed him from worry about whether he'd have work.

He taught me that a man takes pride in his work, whatever it is. He took pride in the quality of his barbering even though barbering would not have been his job in an ideal world. He expected me and my brothers and sisters to take pride in the way we performed our own chores. If the shop windows were streaked after we washed them, or if a school essay had a spelling error, he would fix us with an unhappy look and ask, "Is this the best you can do?" If the front lawn looked sloppy after we cut it, we learned that this was a statement about ourselves. We cut it and raked it again until it made the right statement. He wanted us to do whatever we did with passion for excellence.

He taught us that education and learning how to think were the keys to getting ahead in life. He often went to clinics and demonstrations of new techniques put on by barbering supply companies. If there was a new method of cutting or styling hair, he was determined that he was going to be the first to learn it and the best at doing it. He's a tremendous reader, one of the best-read men I've ever known. He's an analytical thinker. At dinner each night, he dissected our opinions and required us to think if we wanted to justify them.

Truth be told, I was a lot more passionate about sports when I was a kid than I was about studying. My Dad made it clear where his priorities lay. If we wanted to play, we had to bring home report cards that were unblemished by any grades lower than B. He knew that if we put in the effort, we were capable of that and he insisted that we put in the effort. It's no coincidence that all five of his children finished college. Three got their doctorates and taught at the university level and two have become very successful in the business world.

By contrast, perhaps because he knew my passion for sport needed no reinforcement, he never criticized or praised me very much for what I accomplished on the field or in the gym. It was only in high school that I heard, from teammates who got free haircuts from my Dad, that he was proud of what I was doing.

He taught us that pride and self-respect must be earned. We never doubted that we were loved. But we learned that we had to earn respect by giving our best and performing up to our capabilities. My Dad measured our success not so much by what we achieved but by how much we got out of the abilities and opportunities we had. The outcome of the games I played mattered less to him than the effort I put into preparing and performing. He wanted my teams to win if we could, but he cared more that we won in the right way—because we worked hard and played within the rules.

He taught me that there is no such thing as an overachiever. *We are all underachievers. It's just a question of whether we get 40 percent out of the abilities we have or 90 percent.* No one gets one hundred percent, but that was the goal we should strive toward.

We learned the importance of family. Living in Rutland, I was surrounded by uncles and aunts and cousins. They were a huge support group. They cheered our accomplishments. But we also knew that if we ever got in trouble, we would be letting them all down. That was a big responsibility.

Dad was intensely loyal to his family and his friends. If

someone had a problem, he was ready to help. And that problem would stay within the family. Dad didn't believe in speaking ill of a family member outside the family circle. If one of us made a mistake, we knew we'd be reprimanded and punished. But we knew that no one else would hear about it.

He extended that loyalty to his circle of friends and business associates. He always assumed that people were going to treat him decently and honestly until and unless they proved otherwise. We, in turn, extended that loyalty to our friends and our teammates.

He reinforced the lessons we learned in religion classes at school about the centrality of charity. Dad believed that doing well meant doing well by others. If we were making names for ourselves in sports or academics, that just meant that we should be kinder to everyone around us. We had duties to the community. Every Saturday, for instance, it was my responsibility to go to the store and buy groceries for three elderly women, the Manfredi sisters, who lived in the neighborhood. As Dad saw it, I was fortunate enough to be young and healthy. Running errands for those three women was the proper way to use my youth and health.

Dad was a realist. Kids from our side of town, he told us, didn't get the same opportunities and the same breaks that kids from wealthier homes did. Those kids could carouse. They might even take off with a police cruiser, as I remember one kid doing. Their parents could get them off. If we got caught doing that sort of thing, we could expect to be in severe trouble, perhaps in jail. Life, he felt, wasn't always fair, especially in the short run. Other, wealthier people would get more opportunities than we would. So we'd better keep our noses clean, and we'd better be prepared to take advantage of any opportunity that came our way. He had faith that in America, if we did those things, we'd do well. He believed that if we did the right things, if we studied and practiced and looked out for others, good things would happen.

He acknowledged the role of misfortune in the world. He knew that things happen, for better and for worse, that we don't control. He just believed that the harder we worked, the luckier we would be. And he was right.

Dad placed no limits on us and our vision of what we could accomplish. I played basketball for the same school he had attended, Mt. St. Joseph Academy. I was a point guard, and I had few of the obvious talents that you see every night on ESPN. I wasn't tall. I was fast, but not faster than everyone. I was a 50 percent shooter from the floor, but I wasn't a dazzling, long-range gunner. I tried to be the kind of player who did the little things a team needs to win.

When I was a freshman, I went out for the junior varsity at Mt. St. Joseph. I was cut. I wanted to play, so I asked a priest there if I could organize a freshman team. He gave his permission, and the freshman team won the league tournament. I was named most valuable player.

The next year, the same coach who'd cut me reluctantly

kept me on the JV team. But he spoke to my Dad. "Bob isn't going to play very much this year," he said. "And he won't play at all after this year. He just doesn't have enough talent."

My Dad never told me about that conversation until after I had twice been captain of my college basketball team.

It would never have occurred to him to do so, because he knew instinctively the difference between the kind of talent that JV coach appreciated and real talent. He knew that some-one who was persistent, who loved to compete, who was willing to work harder than the competition, had every reason to believe he would succeed.

◆⟨◯

Unfortunately, most people don't have the advantages I had as a boy. Most people are confronted at some early stage in life with a judgment that they don't have the talent to succeed. And most of them accept the judgment. It may come when their score on some standardized test doesn't qualify them for admission to an honors class or a particular college. Or it may come when some coach cuts them from a team and tells them they aren't big enough or fast enough. Whenever it comes, the message that accompanies it is "You're not talented enough to go beyond mediocrity." All too often that message is un-contradicted. Hope dies and people stop trying.

At the other end of the spectrum, a fortunate few are encouraged to believe that they are so talented that their success is all but assured. They have the high SAT numbers, or they have the foot speed, or they have the size that society mistakes for talent.

Quite a few such people wound up at the University of Virginia, where I taught psychology for more than two decades. Virginia is perennially ranked as one of the finest universities in the country, and admission is highly selective. The SAT scores of the entering students are, in fact, one of the key criteria that the rankers use to decide which universities are the best. It's a kind of circular logic.

I wish that the rankers could find a way, instead, to look at how well the students do ten, twenty, or thirty years down the road. I know that they would find that a large percentage of graduates from Virginia, Harvard, and Stanford have fallen way behind a significant number of kids who went to Podunk State, fallen behind them in every conceivable index of success—salary, family life, happiness.

The fact is that the conventional sort of talent measured by the admissions committees at places like Virginia, Harvard, and Stanford matters relatively little when it comes to success in life. Conventional, measurable talent gives you a great chance to be successful, and I'd certainly rather have it than not have it. But conventional, measurable talent might be compared to a person's raw sprinting speed. It's certainly true that if your goal is to become the world champion at 100 meters, it helps to be endowed with raw speed. Practice, conditioning, and good coaching can shave something off an athlete's time for 100 meters, but it won't turn a kid who runs the distance in 12 seconds into a kid who runs it in 9.8 seconds.

But how many of life's endeavors are based on that kind of raw talent? Not many. Even in track and field, a runner who found that he could never run faster than, say, 11 seconds for 100 meters would find that that kind of speed was perfectly adequate for a miler—if he was prepared to commit himself to the training and discipline that it takes to run the mile. Most of the endeavors we undertake in our lives and our careers are much more akin to a mile race—or a marathon—than they are to a 100-meter sprint. *In most of life's endeavors, characteristics like persistence and self-discipline are much more important than the kind of talent measured by standardized tests.* They are some of the characteristics of people with real talent.

That's why success in life correlates so weakly with success in high school. It's why some of the kids at Podunk State are going to outperform some of the kids at Harvard. The kids at Podunk State may have SAT scores of 900 while the kids at Harvard made 1500. But if the Podunk State kids have the character traits that enable them to realize 90 percent of their potential, they will outperform the Harvard kids who lack real talent.

That, I think, is also why some of the great superstars in sport were relatively late bloomers. Michael Jordan and Larry Bird, for instance, were not great basketball players in junior high school. They were small and overlooked. But this forced them to develop a work ethic if they wanted to play. Late in their high school years, when their physical talent bloomed, they already had developed the real talent they needed to become great.

Real talent can be found anywhere. It may even be more likely in a kid at Podunk State, because he realizes that he's got no choice but to develop the characteristics of real talent. The kid at an elite college may have been persuaded that he can coast through life on his IQ scores. I frequently tell students at Virginia that the day after graduation, no one will care where they went to school or what they scored on the SAT. But it takes some of them a long time and some rude surprises to figure out that in the world outside of academia, real talent generally counts a lot more than conventional talent.

❧

Our culture's misperceptions about talent stem, in part, from the drastic wrong turn taken by Western psychology and philosophy for much of this century. A detailed account of this history is beyond the scope of this book. Suffice it to say that when I entered graduate school in the early 1970s, Western thinking about the mind was dominated by the legacies of three men: Sigmund Freud, Alfred Binet, and B.F. Skinner. Freud taught that the character of an adult is the product of childhood events, particularly traumatic events, and of instinctive impulses, or drives. Binet was a French psychologist whose work was fundamental in establishing the notion that intelligence could be measured by standardized tests; one of the most widely used IQ tests was named for him. And Skinner, who taught at Harvard, believed that all human behavior boiled down to conditioned, reflexive responses to certain stimuli. This was a theory he "proved" by attaching electrodes to the brains of mice in devices called Skinner boxes.

In all three of these men's theories, the individual was essentially seen as passive, almost helpless. In Binet's vision, he either had naturally endowed intelligence or he didn't. Skinner perceived the individual as an organism that only responded to stimuli. And Freud thought of us as prisoners of our pasts. They assigned almost no role to concepts like determination and perseverance, which they considered hopelessly old-fashioned and unscientific. Generations of psychologists and psychiatrists who followed Freud, Binet and Skinner took it a step further. Because they couldn't measure the characteristics of real talent, they pretended it did not exist.

Fortunately for me, by the time I got to graduate school I had had a very old-fashioned and unscientific upbringing. The things I learned about real talent from my family in Rutland had been reinforced by skilled teachers and coaches.

After college, I'd had the opportunity to teach swimming and other sports to children with mental and physical disabilities at the Brandon Training School in Vermont. Their success had shown me the critical importance of attitude, rather than so-called talent, in determining whether an individual learns or improves skills. They always had a good attitude, because they were thrilled to have a chance to learn. I was naive enough not to understand that they were too limited to learn. And together, we succeeded.

So when in graduate school I read and heard what Freud, Skinner, Binet, and their disciples had to say, I was skeptical. My skepticism deepened as I looked at the lives of the Freudians and the Skinnerians. Quite often, they had miserable personal lives. They offered a sharp contrast to my parents, to the teachers and coaches I had known in Rutland. In Rutland, the people I respected had offered ways to succeed. In graduate school, I found that the leading lights in the science of the mind all too often were essentially offering rationales for misery and failure. They explained and justified an individual's problems. They had little or nothing to tell someone who wanted solutions, who wanted to lead a happy, successful life.

I found some reinforcement for my skepticism in the works of some earlier psychologists, people who dominated the field before the emergence of Freud, Binet, and Skinner. One of them was William James, the giant of American psychological studies in the latter half of the nineteenth century. James was once asked what psychology had established about the mind in its first fifty years as an academic discipline.

"People," James replied, "tend to become what they think about themselves."

This was the foundation of a psychology I could agree with. Consider its implications. *If you think of yourself as able to*

*do something, you probably will do it. If you think of yourself
as incapable, you probably won't.* If you think of yourself as a
happy, successful person, you probably will be. If you think of
yourself as as an unhappy failure, you probably will be that as
well.

It implied a concept I had long believed in, a concept that
was part of my religious upbringing: free will. *I believe that
every human being has the ability to choose how he thinks
about himself and how he acts.* I believe that this is what
makes humans unique. It is what makes them capable of the
extraordinary.

You can believe that free will is a gift of God if you like. Or
you can believe that free will is an innate human characteristic that developed through evolution. I don't care. But if you
won't believe in free will, if you won't accept the fact that
your mind is your domain, under your control, you might as
well close this book now and give it to someone who does.
Everything I teach, everything I do, is based on the concept of
free will. If you prefer to believe that you are the helpless vic-
tim of circumstances beyond your control, and that these circumstances dictate your behavior, there's not much I can do
to help you. If you believe, as I do, that your past does not have
to be your future or determine your future, there are few limits to what you can achieve.

Free will, combined with James's idea, begins the restora-
tion of the autonomy of the individual to psychology. It liber-

ates us from the shackles of test scores, childhood trauma, and conditioned response to environmental stimuli, the shackles imposed by Binet, Freud, and Skinner.

I was not, of course, the only person entering the field of psychology in the last two decades who had problems with the conventional wisdom. Many psychologists and psychiatrists became skeptical, primarily because they found that Freud, Binet, and Skinner weren't particularly useful if you wanted to help people. Some of them developed a school called cognitive psychology, which is based on the belief that how we perceive our world is critical to the way we feel and act, and that we can control our perceptions. That's a belief I can work with.

My work is a little bit like that of a guide. I help people get to places they couldn't reach on their own. I don't carry them there. I help them find the resources within themselves to make the journey. That's what I hope this book will do for you—to find and develop the real talent that can take you to the places you'd like to reach on your life's journey.

CHAPTER THREE

Do What You Love or Love What You Do

No face symbolizes the resurgence of American business in the last decade more than that of Bill Gates, the co-founder and chairman of Microsoft. I'm by no means a computer software expert, and I'm not in a position to judge Microsoft's product against the products of other companies. But based on what I know about him, Bill Gates's success does not surprise me.

In the late 1960s, when computers were still huge and relatively primitive devices, a company called Computer Center Corporation set up an old PDP-10 mainframe computer in an abandoned automobile dealership in Seattle, where young Bill Gates lived. C-Cubed, as it was known, hoped to rent time on the computer to local businesses.

Gates, at the time, went to a school called Lakeside with an equally primitive computer available to the students, and he had learned some basic programming on it. To give you an idea of what computing was like in those years, the machines at both C-Cubed and Lakeside had no monitors. They operated more or less like teletype machines. And there was virtually no commercially available software. To get the machine to do anything, you first had to write a program telling it what to do.

The kids at Lakeside were hired by C-Cubed and given access to its computer for some tests. C-Cubed wanted to find out what would happen when several users tried to get the computer to work for them at the same time. They invited the boys to do their best to make the computer crash. Bill Gates was very adept at this.

That project ignited a passion in Gates. He was in the eighth grade at the time. His parents, quite wisely, required that he be home in bed at a reasonable hour. But his passion was such that he couldn't obey them. He used to sneak out of his house when the lights were out, climbing through a window. He'd make his way downtown to the old autombobile showroom and that PDP-10 computer. He'd work into the wee hours, trying to figure out how to make that computer do what he wanted it to do. He often worked until after the Seattle buses stopped running and he had to walk home.

Eventually the project ended and the company wanted to charge the Lakeside boys for the use of the machine. Gates found ways to hack into its records and erase the evidence of the boys' use of the computer. He was caught and for the summer between the eighth and ninth grades, he was banned from the premises of the old auto showroom.

But a career had been launched.

Of course, I'm not telling this story to advocate that kids sneak out at night or defraud computer companies. The point is that Bill Gates from the start loved computers and loved writing software. He loved it enough to do it for nothing. He loved it enough to break the rules he lived with in order to do more of it. And that's why it doesn't surprise me that Microsoft has become the giant that it is, or that Gates has become a man who worries about things like how to give away a chunk of the billions he has earned.

Gates and Microsoft love what they do. That, I think, is the main reason they have become wealthy and successful.

And that is one of the first things that separates people with real talent from people without it. *People with real talent do what they love to do.*

They look honestly at themselves. They recognize and acknowledge their own passions. And then they follow them.

Doing what you love solves so many problems. If you do what you love, it's never hard to get out of bed in the morning with a smile on your face. If you do what you love, it will be easy to work as hard as you have to work to succeed. If you'd like a graphic analogy, consider two women with equal physical talents about to compete in the long jump. One of them is wearing shorts, a t-shirt, and track shoes. The other has to wear galoshes and a raincoat, and she has to carry a purse and a briefcase. Who's going to jump farther?

Doing work you dislike is like trying to long-jump in an overcoat and galoshes.

And yet, many people wind up standing at the end of the runway thus encumbered. When I taught at the University of Virginia, I used to get regular visits from kids who would say something like, "Doc, what I really love is zoology and working with animals, but my parents are going to make me go to law school."

Sometimes, I'd ask such a kid whether her parents were happy. Quite often the reply would be that the parents were lawyers or executives who made a comfortable living but weren't living comfortably. They were miserable, and they got through their days and nights with the help of alcohol or Prozac. Or they were grouchy and made the people around them miserable.

I'd remind such a student that her life was her responsibility, not her parents'. She had to take that responsibility, beginning with the choice of what her work should be. And I'd tell her that in my opinion, people who choose to do what they love wind up way ahead of people who don't.

Sometimes, when I state this opinion, someone will reply, "Yeah, Doc, sure. In an ideal world, everyone would do what they love and everyone would make a comfortable living at it. But this isn't an ideal world. I would love to play piano for a living, but I'm not good enough at it. So I do something I don't love because I make good money at it."

Such a person has a point. There are jobs which people love that don't pay a lot of money. I'm thinking, for instance, of public school teachers. No matter how much they love it, no matter how well they do, their salaries are going to be fixed by the board of education. They even must put up with the galling knowledge that excellent teachers are generally paid the same salaries as mediocre ones.

If what you love is teaching in the public schools, you're going to have to accept the fact that you're not going to make as much money as you might in some other field. You have to understand that part of your remuneration will be seeing the positive effect you have on the lives of the children who come through your classroom.

That's not an insignificant reward.

This raises the issue of how success is defined. Is it money? Or is it something else?

I'm not unmindful of the importance of money. And I have no problem with people whose motivation is to earn a lot of money, to provide well, even lavishly, for themselves and for their families. Nor do I have a problem with someone, like a public school teacher, whose motivation is not money. Success is something every individual must define for himself or herself.

Be honest with yourself. If money is important to you,

you're unlikely to be a true success in a profession where the opportunities to earn are limited. On the other hand, if warm relationships with the people you encounter every day are important to you, you're not going to be a true success as head of a collection agency, no matter how much money you make at it.

But it's been my experience that the choices are rarely this stark. In fact, what I usually see is that people generally don't have to choose between money and happiness in their work. The nature of our economy is that you can't do well if you're not supplying something that people need or want. Whether it's good automobiles or astute financial services or wise counsel, people tend to pay well for what they need and want. So if you work well, if you bring something excellent to the marketplace, you're generally going to be paid reasonably well. You may not make Bill Gates's kind of money, but you'll be comfortable.

Someone might respond, "Well, Doc, that's fine for someone still in college. But what about me? I'm in my forties. What I'd really like to be is a novelist, but I sell insurance. I have a wife and two kids who depend on me. I can't just quit my job and start writing novels."

Again, that's a reasonable point. People with families have responsibilities they can't shirk. And I don't advocate that they do so.

But, again, I don't think the choices are as stark as either being miserable selling insurance or becoming a novelist and telling your kids they're on their own for college.

What I might suggest to this wannabe novelist is that he follow the path blazed by Tom Clancy, John Grisham, and others. Clancy wrote *The Hunt for Red October* in the evenings, at his kitchen table, and sold insurance to put food on that table. Grisham wrote *A Time to Kill* while practicing law.

Our wannabe novelist can continue to attend to his business. And he can begin writing novels as a serious hobby. He can take night classes in fiction at a nearby college. He can start the way a lot of novelists start, by getting up early in the morning and writing a couple of hundred words before he goes to work. Or he can throw out the television set and write a couple of hundred words every night after dinner. In this way, he can teach himself quite a bit about the art of fiction.

In the meantime, he can save and invest and take care of his financial obligations to his family as soon as possible. And when those obligations are met, when the last tuition dollar is banked, I would be the first to encourage that person to start trying to write fiction for a living.

By that time, if he's taken part-time fiction seriously, he should have learned a lot about the craft, learned whether he can produce manuscripts that sell, and learned whether he truly loves the work or just likes to daydream about being a literary lion.

People sometimes must set priorities. They can't always

have or do everything that they love at the same time. If a woman came to me and said she dearly wanted to be a successful physician, a mother of two, and a world-class marathoner, and that she loved all three of these dreams equally, I would tell her, "Great." I love to work with someone who has great dreams. But I wouldn't tell her I thought she could do all three of those things at the same time.

She might, for instance, concentrate in her early twenties on establishing her career in medicine. As is the case with a lot of careers, it takes more hours to establish yourself as a doctor than it does to maintain an ongoing medical practice. At the same time, she could take care of her general fitness, running shorter distances. And she could look for a husband who admired her goals and was ready to help her reach them.

Once those elements were in place, she could take some time off to have children. And once the children were in school, she could begin to put in the hours and the mileage necessary to become a world-class marathoner. By that time, of course, she might be in her thirties.

If she objected, "I don't think you can become a world-class marathoner unless you train hard in your twenties," I'd suggest that she might have to put off the children or the career in medicine until she'd seen how good she could be in the marathon. It's her choice. The point is that we must all, at times, choose between things that we love.

Still, there will be people who will read this and object. "Wait a minute, Doc," they'll think. "Your own father's story proves that you can't always make a career doing what you love. He didn't aspire to be a barber. Circumstances forced him into it."

That's true. Though I never heard my father complain about being a barber, I know from the fact that he sacrificed and saved to go to college that he wanted and would have had a different career had the war not intervened.

And I know that there are lots of people who, at some time in their lives, made what they thought were intelligent choices that led them to jobs they don't love but nevertheless want to do well in. Maybe they had a passion for English literature, which led them into teaching, and now they find that they don't really like teaching; it was reading and research that they loved. Or perhaps they saw a chance to achieve financial stability by going to work in the family construction business, but construction doesn't really thrill them.

In fact, there are very few jobs that permit an individual to do solely what he or she loves every minute of every day. There are journalists who love getting out into the field and witnessing history, but hate doing the office politicking and back-scratching they have to do to get those assignments. There are financial consultants who love the satisfaction of helping a client achieve his financial goals, but hate making cold calls. I love the bulk of what I do, which is helping people attain their dreams. But there are aspects of my work—the contracts, the business negotiations, the late connections in dreary airports—that I could do without. Even those of us who love what we do face the challenge of getting enthusiastic about some parts of our jobs.

At such times, I fall back on a bit of wisdom I first heard from the late comedian George Burns: *"You can either do what you love or love what you do. I don't see where there's any other choice."*

That may strike you as a bit fatuous. "No way," you might think, "am I ever going to learn to love what I do. I could no more love my job than I could love lima beans."

If that's the way you choose to think, you're right.

But remember, you have free will. You can choose the way you perceive your work. If you're an English professor, you can choose to perceive your work as marking papers and preparing lectures. Or you can perceive it as helping young people take the same joy from literature that you discovered when you were young. If you're a financial consultant, you can choose to perceive cold calls as the burden of exposing yourself twenty-five times a day to people who say, rather curtly, "I'm not interested and don't call me again." Or you can perceive each unsuccessful call the way Bob Sherman did, as a necessary step in locating the person who's going to give you the profitable satisfaction of helping him or her attain financial security. If you're a lawyer, you can choose to perceive what you do as a mind-numbing slog through old cases that no one cares about anymore. Or you can choose to perceive it as a chance to protect the rights and property of your clients.

This is where one of the home truths I learned in Rutland plays an important role. Happiness comes not so much from doing well, but from doing well by others. If you seek and find the ways in which your work enhances the lives of others, you're going to enjoy it more.

That's a part of why my father never felt any need to complain about what he did for a living. He provided a service that was essential to the health and well-being of the community. He contributed to the quality of people's lives. What he did enabled him to support his wife and children. He learned to love his work for those reasons.

Finally, if nothing else about your job sparks some enthusiasm in you, you can benefit from another of the things I learned from my father. You can do your work well because it's your job. Your performance in it makes a statement about you. You must have pride in that statement. Dad took pride in his skills. That's part of what made him a true professional.

People today sometimes seem to have forgotten this. They do their work sloppily, indifferently. They take no pride in their performance.

Some of these same people will tell me how much they admire athletes, how much they envy them the chance to perform on television every night.

I sometimes think it might be helpful if everyone had to

perform on television. You might start to hear more conversations like this one:

"Honey, I'm home."

"Hello dear. How was your day?"

"Hard day. Hard."

"That's funny. It didn't look very hard on television. You got to the office on time. But from 9:15 to 10:30 all you did was read the paper. Then you made a few calls, but the instant replay showed clearly you were just going through the motions. Then you took a long lunch and came back and played a computer game for half an hour. Then you made a few more calls and piddled around for a while. Then you came home. You call that a hard day?"

It seems to me that more people used to work as if they were on television. They worked as if they were constantly being watched by people whose opinions mattered to them. In fact, they didn't need to be watched. They had pride in what they did. I don't see as much of that pride when I look around today.

I have never tried to prescribe for my clients the method they must use to attain the right state of mind. For example, I generally don't believe it's a good idea for a golfer to watch the scoreboard during a tournament. I think it can distract him from the task at hand, which consists solely of the next shot he must hit. But if a player tells me that knowing where he stands in the tournament helps him focus on that next shot, it's all right with me. He can look at the scoreboard, as long as his results bear out his belief that doing so helps him.

In the same way, I'm not overly concerned with how someone gets enthusiastic about his work. If he gets excited because he loves what he does, like Bill Gates, great. If it's because he's learned to love what he does, that's great, too. And if he gets juiced only because of the pride he takes in the work that he does, that's also fine with me.

I only know that people with real talent find some way to be excited about their work. And they do it every day.

CHAPTER FOUR

Chasing Dreams and Setting Goals

A few years ago, I got a call from a man who had fallen in love with golf. His name was Gary Gersh. One Christmas, several people had given him copies of *Golf Is Not a Game of Perfect*. He'd read it and liked it, and he wanted to talk with me about the ideas in it. He sounded committed to improving his golf game, and I like to work with committed people. So we made an appointment and he came to Charlottesville for a weekend.

As we talked and played golf for those two days, I began to hear things about Gary that reminded me very much of some of the great athletes I've worked with.

Gary could remember one very formative moment in his childhood in Los Angeles. He was about nine years old, and he was listening to the radio. A disk jockey played "Tears of a Clown," by Smokey Robinson and the Miracles. The song blew young Gary Gersh away. "It absolutely captivated me," he says.

Gary became a Motown collector, and there was lots to collect in those years: Smokey Robinson, the Four Tops, Diana Ross and the Supremes. Motown was producing classic songs almost as fast as it was producing cars. Gary couldn't get enough of it. He became a big record collector, branching out from Motown to other labels active in that golden age of rock.

Gary's fascination with music took a slightly different turn than many kids'. He got interested in the people who produced the records, people like David Geffen at Asylum Records and the founder of Motown, Berry Gordy. He read their stories in the pages of *Rolling Stone.* By the time he was thirteen or fourteen years old he knew what he wanted to be. Lying in bed at night, just before sleep, the record player still warm on the table beside him, Gary Gersh dreamed of running a record company.

So he set about trying to break into the business. He wrote to David Geffen at Asylum Records, asking for a chance to go to work. Geffen didn't have any openings for fourteen-year-olds. But when Gary was fifteen he got a job working in a record store. When he was sixteen, he was working in a store called Licorice Pizza. (There's no accounting for some of the things that sounded cool in the 1970s.) The store was starting to expand. He was offered the job of head buyer.

Gary's parents had no more desire than anyone else's parents to see their son stop his education at that age and go to work. They had two other boys who went to law school. But, reluctantly, they tried to understand. Gary left school and went to work.

The dream of running a record company was ever before him, and he jumped in a few years to Capitol Records. He started there at the bottom, as a customer service representative in the promotions department. He visited record stores, putting up posters and counting the items in the sales bins. But he knew from his reading that the heart of the business was finding, evaluating, and nurturing great musicians and songwriters. Within a few years, he edged his way into that.

Over the years, Gary was involved in the careers of the Stray Cats, Nirvana, David Bowie, and Counting Crows. He found that he could trust his instincts in assessing young performers and their songs.

In his early thirties, he landed the job with David Geffen that he'd sought when he was fourteen. And five years ago, he moved from that job to the presidency of Capitol Records, where he'd started at the age of twenty.

✦◇

Gary's judgment, his taste in music, and his personality were all important in his success. But it was his dream that propelled him. And that's why he reminded me of some of the great athletes I've worked with.

Tom Kite is the same way. When he was a young boy growing up in Dallas, Tom used to see the professionals come through town, playing in the forerunner of what is now the

Byron Nelson Classic. He began to dream of being one of them.

Tom held on to his dream in the face of people who told him he was too small, too nearsighted, and not talented enough. He held on to it despite the fact that there was a kid in Austin, his new home, who often beat him. (The kid, of course, was Ben Crenshaw.) Tom persisted in dreaming of himself as a professional golfer, even as a major championship winner.

He held on to that dream through more than twenty years of disappointments in the majors. He held on to it after he hit a ball into the water to lose his lead in the fourth round of the 1989 U.S. Open. He held on to it through hours and days and years of practice under the hot Texas sun, rebuilding his swing so that he would not again hit such a shot under pressure.

And, finally, he won the U.S. Open in 1992.

Tom never counted those hours of practice as work. To him, getting better and chasing his dream are fun. They're what make his life meaningful and satisfying. He's one of the fortunate people, the people with real talent, who have come to realize that no matter what happens in your life, you will come to the end of your days contented if you can truthfully say to yourself that you did the best you could possibly do to attain your dreams.

That's what Tom has in common with Gary Gersh. Dreams.

There's a subtle difference between doing what you love and chasing your dreams. You could, if you loved golf and dreamed of winning the Masters, choose to opt out of competition and become a teaching pro. If you loved the game, you'd probably do well as a teacher. But you wouldn't be chasing your dream.

People who chase their dreams do what they love and they go for greatness. Those kinds of dreams, the dreams that fill their minds with purposeful energy, are the most potent source of motivation I know of.

There's been a tendency in our society in recent years to overuse, distort, and cheapen dreams. Virtually every athlete on television is described as going for a dream. We may soon see actors in commercials pouring the breakfast cereal of their dreams.

But we rarely see the years of sweat and preparation that lie behind the culmination of a dream. On television, we see an athlete on the brink of competition. We hear about the dream. And the next thing we see is the flag going up and the tear in the athlete's eye. The implication is that it's enough to dream of achieving great things—that if you dream, your dreams will somehow come true.

Of course, it doesn't happen that way. *A dream without a commitment is just a fantasy.* People with real talent recognize that. They know that the real heroics occur when no cameras are around, when people keep the commitments they've made and do the work that leads to excellence. They know that real heroes don't simply have dreams. They wake up each morning and find a way to motivate themselves to do what it takes to achieve their dreams.

Dreams and motivation are intertwined. The late Jim Valvano, who coached basketball and won an NCAA championship at N.C. State, used to begin the first practice of each year by having his players cut down the nets. A lot of people would say that cutting down the nets should be the final act of a championship team, not the first act of an unproven one. But Valvano wanted to put a dream in his players' minds.

Gary Barnett, who took Northwestern to its first Rose Bowl in a couple of generations, did something similar. Barnett had roses all over the football area at Northwestern—in his office, on the fence around the practice field. He wanted his players to be thinking constantly about playing in Pasadena.

Jim Valvano and Gary Barnett would have been quite comfortable talking philosophy with William James, the psychologist who said, "People tend to become what they think about themselves." They all understood the importance of dreams.

The kind of dreams I'm talking about, of course, are not the nightmares and fantasies that the subconscious mind pushes forth as we sleep. They're conscious thoughts and aspirations. They are, in James's terms, a form of thinking about yourself.

People with great dreams can achieve great things. People with small dreams can't. If Gary Gersh had seen himself owning a record store instead of running a record company, he would not now be president of Capitol Records. If Tom Kite had dreamed only of someday breaking 80 on the golf course, he would not have won the U.S. Open.

That's because people tend to work as hard as they have to work to achieve what they dream about. If you see yourself as a straight-A student, you're probably going to work harder than the person who thinks she can never be better than a B student. You'd think that it would work the other way around—that a person who saw herself as no better than a B student would be spurred to work harder to compete with those she perceived as more talented. But it doesn't. People do the work required to fill the niche they see themselves occupying. If they can't see themselves accomplishing something, they won't do the work required to accomplish it.

Where do you place yourself? Your self-image is extremely important. It plays a major role in determining your place in life. You need to work on seeing yourself achieving great things.

That's because our culture, rather then encouraging people to dream big and chase their dreams, tends by and large to push them in the opposite direction. Of course, there are exceptions—the occasional motivational speech or sports telecast that highlights the importance of dreams. But arrayed against those exceptions is a steady stream of slights and disappointments that discourage us.

You get cut from a team. Or you don't make the honor roll. You don't make it into your first choice of colleges. You apply for a job and you don't get it. These setbacks sting. The pain is real.

At each of these junctures, there's usually some well-meaning coach, teacher, counselor, or boss who tries to cushion the blow by saying, "Nice try. I'm sure you did your best." The implication is that you're just not talented enough to have aspired to such a level. The suggestion is that you ought to scale back your dreams, diminish your aspirations, and not expose yourself to failure again.

It's a temptation most people succumb to. They find the pain of failure very real. Against it, the potential joy and satisfaction of attaining their dreams seem very ephemeral. So they give up their dreams. They opt for safety and mediocrity. For, after all, if you can't see yourself making the varsity or setting sales records, what's the point of putting in the kind of effort those things would require?

People with real talent, on the other hand, pay no attention to people who question their dreams. When they fail, they pick themselves up and start chasing the dream again. They understand that they will be happy chasing their dreams even if they don't achieve them, because a person who is chasing a dream is a person who is excited, vital, and alive.

I find that these people often feel that they're predestined to accomplish great things. I worked with a golfer who told me that as a kid he used to hum a little song to himself as he practiced. The actual lyrics to the song were "Keep on singing. Don't stop singing. You're gonna be a star someday." But as he practiced, he changed the word "singing" to "swinging." And eventually he did become a star.

Many of the successful black athletes I've worked with at

the University of Virginia had this sense, perhaps because of how far they had come simply to get there. No matter what happened to them, they believed that destiny had chosen them to be the first in their families to get a college degree and to break out of poverty. When you feel that way, a setback becomes just an interesting curve in the road. It's not the end of the road.

~

Despite the power of dreams, most research in the field of psychology tends to ignore them in favor of studying goals. And a lot of companies, who pay for this research, have launched elaborate programs built around goals. It's not because goals are a better motivator than dreams. It's because goals lend themselves to the kind of study that can be done with a No. 2 pencil, quantified, and written up in a professional journal. A dream is too personal, too subjective to lend itself to experimental research.

The import of many of these studies is that the best way to enhance performance is to give an individual a list of difficult but attainable performance goals and to reward him for those that he reaches. This, the studies say, produces better results than simply relying on an individual to do his best.

One problem with those studies is that they usually measure performance on tasks that the subjects don't want to be doing. Frequently it's on something artificial and mindless like replacing blue squares with green triangles. This is supposed to reduce the possibility of some kind of bias entering the study, but it discounts or eliminates the fact that people work best when they're doing something they love and chasing a dream.

Companies use goal-based motivational programs in part because their managers understand that many, if not most, of their employees don't particularly like what they do and aren't chasing dreams. It's easier to set goals for such people than it is to restructure the company so that people with real talent are attracted to it and given the opportunity to work on something they love doing.

For someone whose dreams propel him, these kinds of goal programs are irrelevant at best and a hindrance at worst. I have a friend who's a journalist. He entered the field with dreams of reporting from Washington and overseas, and he went to work with a large organization that had a global network of bureaus.

Shortly afterward, this organization adopted a program called "management by objective." Each reporter was given a series of quotas. Each month, he was supposed to write a certain number of what the organization called "enterprise" pieces, stories which the journalist didn't merely cover but went out and dug up. He had to write a certain number of news analysis pieces. And so on.

This might not have been a bad way to motivate and monitor the performance of some of the people in the organization who weren't going anywhere, the people who had scaled back their dreams and settled for careers with no risk of failure.

But it wasn't necessary for the people who came to the office every day thinking of ways they could write stories that landed on the front page and attracted the attention of the executives who decided on Washington and overseas assignments. These people were thinking about ways to win Pulitzer Prizes, not meet monthly quotas. And on occasion, when they had to interrupt work on a potential prize-winning story to fulfill a quota in another category, they were annoyed. Their respect for the organization diminished.

The goals set by many organizations tend to work the same way. People with real talent often find them annoying. And they're almost always irrelevant to people with real talent because such people set standards for themselves that are far above the goals the company sets. Tom Kite has always told me that a dream is something that feels like his alone. A goal, he thinks, is something someone else has imposed on him. People with dreams generally want only an opportunity to pursue them.

❦

That being said, there are times and places when goals, particularly those that you set for yourself, are appropriate. Take, for instance, a salesman whose performance is not what it should be. Maybe he's abandoned his dreams, or maybe he's gone into sales because he wants to earn more than he could doing something he truly loves. Maybe he's that would-be novelist whose passion is spent on the manuscript he's writing at night and on weekends. But he wants to earn enough to provide well for his family, to take care of his children's education and his own retirement.

It could well be that this salesman thinks he's doing his best when he's at the office. Studies of what psychologists have termed "perceived exertion" show that individuals are not always reliable judges of how hard they're working. There are many people in every organization who think they're working hard, but really aren't if objective measurements are used.

It can be a good idea for such an individual to start setting goals for himself. Maybe the goal is to rack up $2,000 worth of commissions per day—not an abnormally high figure in the financial world. His self-imposed regimen would be to stay in the office each day until he attained that goal.

He could even, as an incentive, allow himself to quit work early whenever he reached that goal before the end of the normal day. Once he got to $2,000 he could turn on the word processor and spend the rest of his time on that novel.

Even if he didn't reach the goal, its existence would have some salutary effects. If enough days ended before he reached $2,000, he would have to start asking himself why. We'll talk about responses to failure in a later chapter. Suffice it for now to say that the goal could help him reevaluate and improve his methods and his work habits.

Goals can be a useful adjunct to dreams. Let's say that your dream is to run in and finish next year's New York Marathon in less than four hours, a pace of slightly more than nine minutes per mile. In order to do that, you might set up a series of monthly goals. By the end of the first month, you'd want to be running three miles every morning at ten minutes per mile. At the end of the second month you'd want to up your daily run to four miles. At the end of the third month, you'd want to reduce your time per mile to 9:45. And so on, until you'd attained your dream.

Successful dreamers use intermediate goals like this all the time. A golfer who dreams of winning his club championship might set a goal of practicing his putting and chipping four times a week for the ten weeks prior to the tournament. A woman who wants to become her club's tennis champion might give herself a goal of hitting a hundred forehands, a hundred backhands, a hundred serves, and a hundred volleys each day in practice. A student whose dream was to win a Rhodes Scholarship might set intermediate goals involving her grade point average and her participation in sports and leadership activities for each semester.

In general, dreams are great motivators for the long run, for a lifetime or a career. Goals are great motivators for the short run, for a day or a week. But I don't really care what an individual uses for motivation, be it dreams or be it goals, as long as he uses something, and it works.

For that to happen, it's important that a person be honest

with himself or herself. Many people aren't. Organizations I've been associated with, like the University of Virginia and Merrill Lynch, generally are quite effective in screening out people who are not very bright. The people within them are capable of figuring out and giving the "correct" answers to questions about their motivation. You would have to look hard at the University or at Merrill to find someone who didn't say that her goal was to be an honors student or a million-dollar producer.

Yet it's quite clear that a lot of people's goals are much lower. Virginia, like any university, has students whose real goals are to have a good time and do just enough work to avoid flunking out. Merrill Lynch, like any business, has people whose real goal is to sell just enough to avoid being called in for a review or fired outright. Many people, consciously or not, set goals that are easy for them, goals they know they'll reach. Their real goal is to avoid giving anyone, including themselves, reason to call them a failure.

I spoke recently with a young man in the investment business. I asked him what his goals were and he mentioned a figure that would put him in the middle of the pack in his office. This young fellow was an excellent golfer, so I asked him to compare the goals he was setting for himself in business with the goals set by my clients on the PGA Tour.

"They've got to be one of the top 125 players in the country just to keep their playing privileges," I reminded him. "Most of them don't even think about that. They're focused on being in the top thirty or top ten in the world. How much would you have to sell if you wanted to be one of the world's top ten in the investment field?"

He blinked. He hadn't thought of his own goals in that context. He realized that he'd been setting goals whose primary virtue was to make him feel comfortable.

For goals to be effective in enhancing performance, they must be challenging. If you can already jog twenty miles, it's not enough to set a goal of finishing a marathon on your feet. If your existing client base generates $250,000 in commissions annually, you're not going to improve your performance much if you set $260,000 as your annual goal.

If your personal goals are truly challenging and you meet them, you won't have to worry much about the goals your organization sets for you. You'll know that you did the best you could do.

People with real talent care about that. And they seem to understand instinctively the importance of setting a dream or a goal in front of themselves and using it for motivation.

When Gary Gersh, the president of Capitol Records, contacted me it was not to talk about his dreams of success in the record business. It was about a new dream he had. The dream involved a four-day tournament called the Kelly-Barruck Pebble Beach Invitational. It's an event held each year on some of the great Monterey Peninsula courses in California, including Pebble Beach. The players are all part of the entertainment industry. "It's kind of my Masters," Gary says.

Though he hadn't done well the first few times he played, Gary wanted to win it. In effect, he selected a new dream for himself, a dream that would serve the same function in his golf game that his childhood dream of running a record company had served in his career. The dream prodded him to work hard on both the mental and physical aspects of his game. He got instruction on his short game. Together, we worked on developing a confident putting routine.

It paid off the next year at Pebble Beach. Gary, who carried a handicap of 12 at the time, shot some excellent rounds. He had an 85 at Pebble, an 89 at Spanish Bay, and a marvelous 80 in the rain at Spyglass Hill. After three rounds, he led the net score standings by eight strokes.

He called me up that night and asked me for advice. He thought, he told me later, that I had some secret key I could give him, a little bit of mental prestidigitation that winning golfers use when they're trying to sleep with a big lead on the night before the final round of a major championship.

There was no secret, I said. He just had to play one shot at a time and have fun.

The next day, Gary didn't have the same game he had the day before at Spyglass Hill. He had to struggle to make bogies on the first six holes. He kept calm, kept playing one shot at a time, and did well on the next five holes. Standing on the tee at No. 13, he still had an eight-stroke lead. He knew because he was playing in the same group with his closest pursuers.

The next two holes were nightmares. He hit out-of-bounds on No. 13 and took a triple-bogey. He did the same thing playing No. 14, a long par five into the wind. His lead was down to two shots. Then he hit his drive behind a tree on No. 15.

Gary's caddie suggested he chip out and try to assure a bogey. It wasn't bad advice. But Gary was too close to his goal to take it. He took a 7-iron and hit a deliberate cut that curved around the tree, hit the green, and settled a few feet from the pin. He made his birdie, picked up another stroke at No. 16, and was able to make a seven on No. 18 and still win the tournament by two.

Walking up the fairway on No. 18 at Pebble, with the ocean on his left, his mind filled with thoughts of the great golfers who had played and won on the same turf, was an experience he won't soon forget. "It was as good as it gets," he told me later.

Perhaps it was. But it was not a unique feeling. In fact it's a feeling that people who chase their dreams and people who set challenging goals for themselves get to experience more often than you might think.

CHAPTER FIVE

The Success Process

During the years I was associated with the University of Virginia basketball team, the man we most wanted to beat was Dean Smith of the University of North Carolina. The Tar Heels under Coach Smith exemplified consistent excellence. Every year, you knew that his team would play tenacious defense, pass the ball unselfishly, and make its free throws in the final seconds. Not only that, but you couldn't dismiss North Carolina as some bandit school that won by bending the rules. You knew the Tar Heels would do it with players who went to class, stayed out of trouble, and graduated. Every year, you knew that if you could beat North Carolina, you had indeed accomplished something important. Of course, it didn't happen often enough to suit us.

Now that he's retired, it's a little easier to see how much Coach Smith gave to us and to everyone else in the Atlantic Coast Conference. His teams forced everyone on North Carolina's schedule to stretch themselves. We thought constantly about how we could meet the competitive standard he set. We worked harder to try to do it. He was a role model who improved us all.

I recall being especially impressed by the strength of Coach Smith's system. His teams had some great individuals, starting with Billy Cunningham and going on down through Michael Jordan and Antawn Jamison. But the program didn't falter when a superstar graduated. New stars emerged, until it became clear to everyone that the real star was Coach Smith. Obviously, he was following a plan that produced consistent excellence.

Since he retired, I've had a chance to ask Coach Smith a little about that plan and he's been kind enough to share some information about it.

It began with the players he recruited. North Carolina had its standards for academic ability and physical talent. But it also had standards for real talent. Coach Smith stopped recruiting players if he found their work ethic suspect or their character lacking in some other way. (We'll talk more about identifying and recruiting real talent in a later chapter.) He told me he liked to recruit "gym rats," players who like nothing better in their spare time than getting into a gym and working on their skills.

But Coach Smith did not limit himself to recruited players. He welcomed walk-ons as well. In the parlance of college sport, a walk-on is an athlete who isn't recruited because he wasn't considered good enough for a scholarship. He tries out for the team anyway. A lot of coaches disdain walk-ons. They look at them only when they're desperate because their scholarship players have gotten injured, flunked out, or transferred. But I've noticed that good coaches (including Virginia football coach George Welch) like to give walk-ons a chance.

"From day one, we've had at least one walk-on on the team," Coach Smith told me. "We had to when I first started. We didn't have enough scholarship players. But I found that they helped make sure the team was a part of the student body. And the effort they put out just to make the team and have a chance to play was obvious."

To be sure, Coach Smith never relied on walk-ons to form the bulk of his team after his first season. But he was delighted when they could contribute despite their physical limitations. It's still very easy, for instance, to get him to talk about the defensive job a walk-on named Mickey Bell did on the great David Thompson of N.C. State in the 1975 season.

The North Carolina walk-ons clearly had to have more real talent than physical talent. Even when they didn't play that much, I suspect that their determination, enthusiasm, persistence, and optimism made a greater contribution to the Tar Heels over the years than most people imagined, if only for the example they set in practice. They became one way that Coach Smith taught his players about the importance of real talent.

Once he had selected his players, Coach Smith followed a

process designed to mold them into excellent teams. Every year, he told his players the same thing. "Number one, we're going to play hard. No one's going to play harder; at least, that's the goal. Number two, we're going to play together. Number three, we're going to play smart. We're going to execute."

Of course, a lot of coaches try to instill these ideas in their players. No one did it as well for as long as Coach Smith. Part of his method was the way he conducted practice. North Carolina workouts were arduous and competitive. Once he had taught his players a drill, Coach Smith turned the drill into a game. The losing side in a drill had to run. So practice simulated game pressure.

Those pressurized drills were one thing that told Coach Smith that Michael Jordan was developing into the great player he became. Though he hit the winning shot in the NCAA title game as a freshman, Jordan did not make any pre-season All-America teams before his sophomore year. But when he reported to practice, the coaches noticed that he had changed. He had grown another inch. His body had matured. And he still had the ferocious competitiveness and motivation he had developed as a younger, smaller player.

"One day in fall drills that year," Coach Smith told me, "Michael whispered to one of the assistant coaches, 'My side's not going to run all fall.' [By that, Jordan meant that his group would never have to do the penalty laps for losing in a three-on-three drill.] And when the coaches thought back on it, they realized that Jordan hadn't run in three weeks of practice until that time." That was how much North Carolina's practice drills inspired Jordan's competitive nature.

Coach Smith also had customs designed to inculcate the primacy of the team. No matter how highly recruited a high school player was, for instance, he had no right to his favorite jersey number when he came to Chapel Hill. Numbers were handed out on a seniority basis. Seniors chose, then juniors, and so on. And whenever a North Carolina player came out of a game, his teammates on the bench stood and applauded him. These were small things that Coach Smith insisted on. It was only recently, listening to a sociologist give a lecture, that he realized they could be considered bonding rituals which drew his teams closer together and perhaps inspired that extra pass to the open man that characterized North Carolina's offense.

Obviously, there was more—much more—to Dean Smith's system than recruiting gym rats, welcoming walk-ons, competitive practice drills, and customs that stressed the primacy of the team. I cite these not to give an exhaustive account of Coach Smith's methods, but to make a point about people with real talent:

When people with real talent approach any endeavor, they look for a method, a process, that will lead to success. Then they follow that process every day. They set themselves up to succeed.

Dean Smith never picked up a basketball on the first day of

fall practice and asked himself, "What will I do with the boys this year?" He had a system, a set of principles, and a process. He picked up a lot of it from his father, a high school coach. He learned more from Phog Allen at the University of Kansas. Some of it he devised himself. And he stuck with that process. He stuck with it in the early years, when students hung him in effigy during a losing streak. He stuck with it when his teams lost in the Final Four. He stuck with it when he had players like Michael Jordan and won NCAA titles.

He was not inflexible. In the early years, he told me, he used to have competitive free throw practices where the whole squad had to run if a player missed a foul shot. He reasoned that this would toughen players' minds for clutch situations at the end of games when they didn't want to let the team down. But after a year in which North Carolina missed some key free throws, he thought about that aspect of the system again. He decided that punishment running only etched the missed practice free throw into a player's memory. He wanted his players to have positive, confident thoughts when they went to the line. So he changed that particular element of his practice process.

The basic elements, though, remained constant. You could watch a North Carolina team in the 1960s, go off to Siberia for thirty years and return to see a North Carolina team play in the 1990s. You'd know that the same man coached both teams.

Virtually any job, any endeavor, can be attacked this way, through a well-conceived process. It's certainly true in golf. The successful players with whom I work have all committed themselves to one or more processes.

The golfer's process begins with basic fitness. Nearly every winner on the Tour these days follows a fitness program that's designed to keep him strong and flexible. Almost everyone watches what he eats. They see that this is one of the things that successful players tend to do.

The next step is preparation and maintenance of the golfer's game. If you play golf, you already know some of the basics. It's not enough just to go to the range occasionally and hit some drives. You have to practice on a regular schedule. You have to attend to details like the percentage of your practice time you spend analyzing and criticizing the mechanics of your swing versus the percentage of time you spend trusting your swing. (For more on this, see *Golf Is Not a Game of Perfect.*) Most important, you have to devote the majority of your practice time to the portions of the game that are most vital to scoring. For the bulk of the golfers I work with, this is the short game—the little chips, pitches, and putts taken around the green and the hole. Every job, every business has an analogous area that requires special attention, that is most critical to success.

For most golfers, the preparation and maintenance process

includes taking regular breaks from the Tour to rest and review the fundamentals with their swing teachers. They need regular checks to make sure they are still correctly doing the things they first learned years ago—the grip, the stance, and so on. Good players strive to catch and correct immediately any small imprecisions that creep into these areas. The same is true for attitude. The great performers constantly monitor themselves and correct their attitudes when they get half an inch from a great frame of mind. Lesser performers wait until their minds are miles away from where they should be and they've been in a bad mood for weeks before they do anything to correct the situation.

Next, great golfers commit themselves to a routine they will use for every shot in every competitive round they play. The routine is a process designed to clear the golfer's mind of distractions and focus it on the shot at hand. It may include elements like selecting a target, taking a practice swing, and visualizing the shot the player wants to hit. (Again, if you're a golfer and you want more detailed information about routines, read *Golf Is Not a Game of Perfect*.) The routine can't be something a golfer holds in reserve for stressful situations. If he did, it wouldn't be effective. Routines help, in part, because they are the same for every shot. They are intended to produce the same feeling of calm purposefulness whether the golfer is hitting his first putt on Thursday morning or the last putt on Sunday afternoon with all of the money on the line.

People with real talent check with experts to make certain their processes are sound. Then they invest faith, patience, and commitment. That's what David Duval did.

I first met David nearly a decade ago when he was a student at Georgia Tech. David had the good fortune to play for Puggy Blackmon, one of the most caring and dedicated coaches in the country. Puggy is now building a successful program at the University of South Carolina, but he was then the Tech coach. He employed me for several days each year as a consultant to teach his players about sound mental approaches to the game.

David was already a solid golfer when I met him. He hit the ball long and straight, he putted well, and he believed in himself. But the transition to college golf wasn't always smooth and easy for him. He had to hone his mental skills, improving his confidence, his game planning, his sense of strategy. He had to learn to keep his mind focused in the present on the golf course, on the stroke at hand. That meant he had to let nothing bother him. He had to develop sound routines for every part of his game. He didn't win regularly till his senior year.

He had to develop still further when he turned professional, doing all of these things still better and more consistently. Again, the transition wasn't completely smooth. He missed the cutoff score at the PGA Tour Qualifying School and had to reconcile himself to a stint on the Nike Tour while college rivals whom he'd dominated were playing on the big tour. Eventually, he became one of the leading money winners on the Nike circuit.

When he reached the PGA Tour he found immediate, but not complete, success. He set a rookie earnings record with $881,436 in 1995. He made the President's Cup team in 1996 and went 4-0 in his matches. But he didn't win any tournaments. He finished second seven times. Occasionally he made mistakes in the final round. More often, he played well but someone else played better.

At the PGA Championship in Louisville in 1996, David was discouraged. It was broiling that week. David told me he was exhausted by the heat and humidity. He said he didn't ever again want to play golf in late July and August because it took so much out of him.

"It seems to me you have two choices," I said. "You can play more events early in the year and play well enough that you can afford to take six weeks off in July and August. Or you can get into better physical condition so the hot weather doesn't wear you out."

David thought about it for a little while and then committed himself to making enhanced fitness part of his fundamental process. Over the next year he exercised and lifted weights on a regular basis. He got stronger and leaner. He lost about thirty pounds.

But he still didn't win. In the fall of 1997, we talked at Kingsmill, where David was preparing to play in the Michelob Classic. He told me he'd been hearing a lot of suggestions and criticism. Some people were telling him that lifting weights had damaged his touch around the greens. Others said he'd lost too much weight. Still others said he needed to change his grip. David was having a hard time ignoring them, a hard time keeping faith that his improvement process would work.

"Listen, you son-of-a-buck," I said. "I've been watching the way tournament winners prepare themselves for a long time. Don't even think about stopping exercising or changing your grip. You're doing exactly the right things. Your process is sound. Winning just hasn't happened yet, and I don't know why. But the good news is that it will happen. Part of a great career is the wins you record. But another part is all the seconds and fifths and top tens. You're piling those up now and you'll add the wins later. Don't try to fix something that's not broken."

I cited lots of examples for him. Ben Hogan was perhaps the most famous. For years he stuck with a process of improving his swing even though it didn't win him much. He was meticulous about the way he practiced and the frequency of his practice. He left nothing to chance. Before each tournament he played solitary practice rounds, mapping every hole and planning every shot. For a long time, he seemed like an odd-ball loser. But finally, after he'd been barely scratching out a living as a pro for nearly ten years, it started to come together for him. When it did, Hogan didn't change. He stayed with the process that brought him success. Only this time, no one laughed. Young pros gathered round to watch him practice.

They trailed behind him inconspicuously as he played his practice rounds, watching how he scouted a course. Hogan's process became the standard for a generation.

David knew that the fundamentals he'd learned from his father, Bob, were sound and right for him, including his grip. He believed in his mental approach to the game. He knew fitness was an asset. He just had to be patient, as Hogan was.

In a sense, he had to redefine success. For him, success had to be doing the things that would lead to winning, doing them diligently, doing them every day. He had to be patient, but he had to be patient while adhering to the process that leads to success. *Patience alone doesn't get you anywhere. You have to be patient while doing the right things.*

Anyone, in any endeavor, can profit from this principle. Define the process that leads to success. Learn to love the process. Be committed to it. Be patient while you wait for it to work. Define success in terms of how well you honor your commitment to the process.

Fortunately, David stayed the course. And that week at Kingsmill, everything fell into place for him. He won the Michelob in a playoff with Duffy Waldorf. Then he won the Disney tournament in Orlando in a playoff with Dan Forsman. And he finished his season by winning the Tour Championship, making it three wins in three starts. More recently, he won the Tucson Open, the Houston Open, repeated his triumph at Kingsmill, and won the World Series of Golf.

The media, of course, wanted to know what David had

changed to make himself a winner. Many reporters weren't happy with his answer, which was that he had changed nothing. They would have preferred that he confide that some quick fix had helped him, some tip they could pass along to their readers. David's answer didn't make a good story, but it was truthful. He had simply stuck with a process he knew would lead to success. He had been patient in waiting for it to happen. In fact, his patience was such that he stopped practicing just for the sake of going out and hitting balls after every round. He practiced only as much as he needed to. He was, therefore, fresher and more composed in competition.

Reporters with real talent, the ones who succeed by following a sound journalistic process, recognized the validity of his answer.

The fact is that it would be very difficult to fail, no matter what your endeavor, if you went to work every day with a great attitude and dedicated yourself to a sound process. Whether your line is hitting golf balls or teaching school, the principle is the same.

A great attitude means, to borrow a sports expression, that you're juiced every day about the process. You're not just going through the motions. You treat every step of the process as if it's the one that, properly done, could lead to the success you've dreamed of.

This isn't easy. Most of the time, in most jobs, no one but you will know whether you're really engaged in the process or just faking it. If you're a golfer, reporters won't consider your great attitude a hot story, because they can't really see it. Take two golfers on a practice green. Both are stroking putts. But one of them is really concentrating, thinking about his putting routine, trying to execute every practice putt as if a tournament depended on it. The other is daydreaming. To a reporter behind the ropes, they both look like they're practicing. But only one of them really is.

It's the same in most businesses. Some salesmen are at the top of their form on every call. Some sound bored and give the customer the impression they're waiting, even eager, for rejection so they can get back in their cars and go home. They all pay lip service to a sales process, but only some are engaged in it.

Goals, as noted in the last chapter, can be an integral part of immersion in a process. You'll recall that goals work best when applied to short-term tasks. Dreams work best as long-term motivators. People with real talent constantly use goals to make sure that they're truly immersed in a process.

Take a young football player whose dream is to get to the National Football League. He knows that he has to get stronger to do that, and he knows that the weight room is the place he can get stronger. So he sets goals for his weight-training program. Perhaps he starts the off-season able to do ten repetitions with 200 pounds in the bench press. His goal may be to do that with 300 pounds by the time the next season starts.

He may set intermediate goals along the way—so many

pounds and so many reps by the end of the first month, and so on. And he has a slew of other goals relating to the process of improving as a football player. Fifty 100-yard wind sprints four days a week. Getting his time under five seconds for the 40-yard dash. If he's a passer he may throw 500 balls a week. If he's a receiver he may find someone to throw that many to him. All of this is by way of ensuring that he's fully engaged. There are no medals to be won in the bench press. But improving strength is one of the processes football players use to get better.

That illustrates a key aspect of processes that lead to success. Most often, they have more to do with how an individual prepares himself, how he betters himself, than they have to do with how he performs in a specific competitive situation. The process of winning football games may end with catching a touchdown pass in the stadium in front of a big crowd. But it begins in the weight room, working by yourself to make your body stronger. In the same way, the process of winning golf tournaments may culminate in hitting fairways and greens and sinking putts from Thursday to Sunday. But it has a lot more to do with time spent before competition at the driving range and on the practice green and in the fitness trailer.

It's the same way in business. I once asked Phil Blevins of Merrill Lynch about the process that makes financial consultants successful. Phil is better qualified than almost anyone to answer the question. When he started as manager of Merrill Lynch's Washington, D.C., office in 1978, it had two brokers. Today it has more than 150, and it is the second most successful retail brokerage office in the history of the financial business (behind only Merrill Lynch's home office in New York). He knows what works.

I expected Phil to answer by saying something to the effect that successful brokers study the market and the economy for good investments, compile lists of prospects, call on the prospects, and keep doing it until prospects become clients. Then they service the clients assiduously.

But that's not what Phil said. Successful brokers, he told me, follow a process that focuses first on themselves and their own attitudes and skills. Some of it is relatively obvious and superficial. Phil believes, for instance, that if you want people to entrust their money to you, you had better look the part of a trustworthy individual. You wear suits, not sportcoats. You keep your shoes shined. And you have an office environment that is orderly and reassuring, with a kind of calm energy to it.

Phil's insistence on this extends even to the custodial staff. The first time I visited his office, I arrived at about 6:45 A.M. for a 7:30 meeting because I overestimated my travel time. Phil hadn't arrived yet. Neither had any of the brokers. But it didn't take ten seconds for one of the custodians to spot me, welcome me, offer me coffee and a breakfast roll, and assure me I was in competent hands.

Next, Phil says, a good broker focuses on his or her own attitude. Do you get up each morning feeling energetic, enthused, and tenacious? If you don't, you had better find a way to start feeling that way. Phil himself has discovered that reading biographies helps him do this. He's constantly going through the lives of successful people, from Vince Lombardi to Harry Truman, looking for traits and attitudes that he can apply to his own work.

Then it's a question of having faith in the products you're selling. You have to believe that the securities Merrill Lynch's research department recommends will be good investments for your clients. Doubt about the product seeps into a sales effort and ruins it.

Successful brokers, Phil has found, constantly monitor and hone their personal skills and their business skills. They understand that they have to find ways to engage prospects. They have to be likable. They have to be trustworthy. They work on trying to figure out how different clients express their needs and how they respond to those needs. There are some general principles in this. Prospective clients tend to respond well to a broker who is genuinely interested in them, in their ideas, in their aspirations and dreams. If a broker can find out what a prospect truly wants and needs, he is halfway to making the prospect a client.

But each prospect is different, and a successful broker learns to size up prospects and evaluate their differences almost instantly. The analogy to pitching is an appropriate one. A good baseball pitcher learns to derive enormous amounts of useful information from what he observes as a batter takes his stance—the way he stands, the way he holds the bat, the look in his eyes. He adds to this his knowledge of the game situation. He tailors his pitches accordingly. A top professional broker, similarly, learns to react to any situation and use the training and skills he's developed to give him an advantage over competitors who haven't been as conscientious about a sound process.

A successful broker trains himself to stay in the present, focusing on the task at hand rather than what happened during his last call or what he hopes will happen at the end of the day. He disciplines himself to be stable emotionally, not getting too excited about a successful call or discouraged about an unsuccessful one.

These personal improvement processes are the top priority, Phil says. Only when they are taken care of does the successful broker attend to what an outsider might consider the first priority, which is studying the market and the economy for good investments. It's great, Phil thinks, to know the political status of the Russian oil industry and how that will affect bond prices. But the knowledge doesn't do you much good unless you have the right demeanor and the right attitude.

And only after these personal improvement and knowledge-building processes have been attended to does the broker focus on the process of finding prospects and calling on them. At that stage, Phil says, there is no single method that leads to success. Some brokers find clients by cold-calling names on a list. Some hold seminars and invite the public. Some call on small-business owners. Some work with accountants and attorneys. A few play golf and find clients at the club. Most do a combination of one or more of these things. And they all follow up with personal attention to a client, staying in touch with the client's changing needs and desires. But it's not as cut-and-dried as following the instructions for assembling a model airplane. Processes that work for one broker may not suit another. Processes that work with one group of prospects may not work for another.

And the main thing is always the broker's own readiness. "The best financial consultants I've observed spend a lot of time developing themselves," Phil says. "They're constantly managing themselves, working on themselves to be better."

I've noticed this trait among top performers in every business I've been associated with. They all manage themselves carefully. They all have routines designed to assure that they are personally prepared as well as possible to do their best every day. At night, they clear their minds before they go to sleep. They start gearing up mentally for their work when they step into the shower. They accelerate this process of mental preparation as they ride to work. When they get to the office, they are ready to go. They don't let their attitudes depend on how they felt when they woke up, or how the first couple of calls or meetings went. All day, they follow processes and routines designed to assure peak productivity. Then, when they leave the office, they leave work behind and shift their attention to family and recreation.

They understand that the process, the routine, that leads to success in business must be one that engages and affects the mind. It's not enough to go through the motions physically, any more than it's enough for a golfer to execute the movements of a routine when his mind isn't on the golf course. To be at your best, you must routinely commit yourself to being in a great frame of mind for every hour of every business day. Not only will this enable you to perform at your peak but it will also affect the way your customers, clients, and colleagues perceive you. Don't forget that no one is interested in the excuses you might have for being in a foul mood, any more than the sports world cares about the excuses a golfer might have for playing without concentration and desire. You want the people around you to come to value you for the reliability of your optimism, confidence, and enthusiasm.

You want them to perceive that you're an individual who sets himself up to succeed. Like Dean Smith and David Duval, you must have a process you believe in, and you must recommit yourself to it every day.

CHAPTER SIX

Honoring Your Commitments

I once wrote that playing golf confidently was a matter of "playing with your eyes," of seeing where you wanted the ball to go and letting your body and your skill send it there. That was before I met Pat Browne. Pat plays golf, and plays it very well, without seeing. How he learned to do that demonstrates the way people with real talent make and keep commitments to themselves.

Pat lives in New Orleans, where he grew up. His forebears were Irish immigrants who got off the boat in Mobile, Alabama, and created a place for themselves in the New World in a variety of businesses, from wholesale groceries to brewing beer to practicing law. Pat is tall and rawboned with a genteel manner and a deep drawl, and he was a talented athlete as a young man. He played basketball for Tulane. He was the captain of the team in his junior and senior years, and he set a school scoring record of 33 points in a game against Georgia.

In the spring, he was also captain of the Tulane golf team. At his best, he carried a two handicap.

He finished law school at Tulane and became a trial lawyer. He continued to play golf on weekends, but his handicap rose to about seven.

When he was thirty-two, he was returning to New Orleans from a wedding in Baton Rouge on a road called the Airline Highway. A cousin was driving. A car heading for Baton Rouge veered out of control, jumped the median, and struck the car Pat was in. The hood of the car came through the windshield, smashing Pat's face and shoulders.

When he regained consciousness, he could not see. He also had a broken jaw, a dislocated shoulder, a broken collarbone and kneecap, and a faceful of glass fragments. The trauma to his chest was severe enough that his heart stopped a few times and had to be restarted with electric paddles. He recalls awakening in a hospital room to the voice of one of his law partners. He asked the man to cover a deposition he was supposed to take the next day in Birmingham.

Pat remained in the hospital for several months while the doctors plucked glass from his face and repaired his shattered bones and teeth. But while the doctors often shone light in his eyes in the hope that his optic nerve was not completely severed and his sight might be coming back, Pat saw nothing. He realized early on that he would be blind for the rest of his life.

When the hospital finally released him, he set about restoring that life. He learned to navigate with the help of a cane and his friends. He got used to taking someone's right arm and letting that person guide him through rooms and along sidewalks. He got some instruction in the little tricks that the blind use to get through the day, like having someone sort their socks and put them together with rubber bands so that they'll always have a matching pair. He developed a bit of what some blind people call "facial vision," which is the ability to sense the presence of walls and other large impediments by the way sound bounces off of them. He learned to recognize people by their voices rather than their faces.

"It never occurred to me that I wouldn't be able to get back to being a trial attorney," he says. He did that by focusing not on his misfortunes, but on his blessings. He was blessed, he said, with a secretary who had the patience and skill to read to him. He'd been blessed with a Jesuit high school education that had required him to memorize information. So he learned to master the facts in a case by having them read to him or listening to witnesses giving depositions. He absorbed what he heard. "It's not that blindness makes your hearing more acute," Pat says. "It's that you pay much closer attention to what you hear."

Soon, Pat was trying cases again. Sometimes, he'd stand to address the jury and unwittingly face the wrong way. A partner would have to orient him in the right direction. But he was always thoroughly prepared and quick to catch inconsistencies in testimony. Once again he was earning his living.

He set about restoring his body as well as his career. While his injuries were healing, he'd been subsisting on a liquid diet because of his broken jaw. He'd lost about fifty pounds from a lean frame. With a friend named Donald Doyle, he returned to Tulane and put himself under the direction of the athletic department trainer, Bubba Porche. He did sit-ups and push-ups. He circled the Tulane track with Doyle a step ahead, first walking, then jogging. Gradually, he got fit.

And finally, he returned to golf. It began casually, about eighteen months after the accident. A couple of friends took Pat out to New Orleans Country Club, his home course, and led him to the range. They put a driver in his hands and placed a ball on a tee in front of the clubhead. Pat swung. He doesn't recall too much about that first shot, except that he made some kind of contact with the ball. By the end of that session he had hit at least one ball solidly. That was enough to let him see the possibilities in seeing with his mind's eye.

That one solid shot told Pat that he could learn to play again. He knew his body was capable of swinging the club pretty well. It was a matter of finding ways to overcome the obstacle of blindness.

To someone who has never seen blind golfers, this may seem incredible. But they can and do play golf, with the help of coaches—if they're willing to make and honor the commitment required to learn to play without sight.

Pat, with the help of a law partner named Henry Sarpy, made that commitment. It was not an easy process. In blind golf, the coach and the player are equal partners. The coach leads the golfer to the ball. He describes the situation the golfer faces. He helps the golfer line himself up. He puts the clubhead down behind the ball. Then he steps away and the golfer swings. The coach describes the flight of the ball. Then the process begins again.

Pat and Henry worked out an efficient system for doing this. Once he's close to the ball and his coach has described the situation he's facing, Pat and the coach agree on a club. The coach puts it in his hands. Pat lays the shaft of the club along his thighs and the coach presses on it until the shaft is parallel to the intended line of flight. This lines up Pat's body and feet. Once that's done, Pat must remain still while the coach places the clubhead behind the ball. He can't take a waggle after the coach moves because he might not bring the clubhead back to the right spot. He swings from a full rest.

On the greens, Pat and his coach walk a line close to and parallel to the line of the putt. Pat gets a feel for the slope of the green and the distance to the hole with his feet before he lines up. Here, his coach has to be creative. If there's a downhill slope, he might tell Pat to hit a 12-foot putt even if the putt has to travel fifteen feet. The system, of course, is based on the fact that Pat has spent countless hours in practice until he knows precisely how hard to hit the ball to make it travel 12 feet.

It's a system that requires a lot of the coach, and Pat has been blessed with some loyal friends who have shared the job over the years. Henry Sarpy spent many hours with Pat in his early years. After Henry married and started a family, a young man named Gerry Barousse became Pat's prinicipal coach. There have been many others, but as this is written, Pat's son Patrick, who is seventeen, is taking over the job.

Watching Pat and Patrick practice, several things become apparent. The first is that Pat distills an enormous amount of information from what he hears and feels. He can tell by the sound of a ball on a clubhead whether someone's hit the ball straight or off-center. He can tell by the way a shot feels to his hands whether he's hooked or sliced. Although Patrick describes each shot to him, Pat usually knows what's happened as soon as the ball leaves the clubface. The second thing is that Pat is just a golfer, like anyone else. After watching him for a while, you almost forget that he's blind. He becomes just another sixty-five-year-old with a sore left shoulder trying to square his clubface and stop pushing the ball.

Of course, years of practice and commitment have gone into making him this way. The first summer with Henry Sarpy, Pat worked on the practice range for a couple of hours a day, every day. He had to learn to hit shots, especially chips and pitches, not in response to a visual target, but in response to a number. If his coach told him the flag was 60 yards away, he had to produce a swing that sent the ball 60 yards. It took a lot of time and sweat. But Pat made a commitment to restore his golf game, and he kept that commitment.

There were several factors behind this. One is the strong work ethic Pat's father instilled in him. Another is his good sense of humor. He was able to laugh at himself when things went wrong. He encouraged his friends at the club to treat him as they always had, teasing and joking. A third was Pat's ability to find reasons for optimism some people would miss. He will never, he points out, be intimidated by the sight of a greenside pond or a yawning bunker. A 150-yard approach shot is the same to Pat on the range as it is on a course strewn with hazards. And he loved the game.

But the most important factor, I believe, was the self-image Pat held in his mind. He never stopped seeing himself as good enough to get back to playing with his regular foursome at New Orleans Country Club. After a while he heard about national competitions for blind golfers. He saw himself as good enough to win those. And those images sustained him and his commitment through the inevitable setbacks that come to any golfer. The irony behind Pat Browne's golf game is that despite his blindness, the picture in his mind's eye was bright and enduring.

That self-image, I think, is what enables some people to maintain and honor the commitments they make while others falter and give up. The ones who maintain their commitments are sustained by a vision of themselves as they would like to be. The ones who falter are those who rely on progress to sustain their motivation. When progress stops, so does their commitment.

Take, for instance, one of the most common commitments people make, a commitment to physical fitness. Most often, this begins on a fairly arbitrary date, like New Year's Day or a month before the beginning of tennis season.

This commitment causes the people who make it to begin dieting and jogging or going to a health club. But within a few weeks, most of them give up. They go off their diets, they stop exercising, and they revert to their old ways.

That's because most people rely on daily reinforcement for motivation. They can stick with a diet as long as the scale keeps telling them that they're losing weight. They can stick with an exercise program as long as they see that every day they're running a little farther or faster or lifting a little more weight.

But there are few, if any, human endeavors that offer steady, daily progress. If you're trying to lose weight, you're going to hit some plateaus where the scale keeps giving you the same number, or a higher number, even though you've been eating properly. If you're trying to jog, there will be weeks when you just won't run as far or as fast as you did the week before. Pat Browne went through many periods like this with his golf game. Even though he was practicing diligently, he'd unwittingly let something in his swing slip out of place. He'd open his shoulders a bit or change his stance. And the ball would start flying sideways. Pat would go backwards.

This is when most people stop honoring their commitments and quit. It's when people with real talent keep going.

The ability to make and keep commitments to yourself is

critical. In most endeavors, it's what separates the successful from the mediocre.

If you are the type of person who has trouble keeping commitments to processes that will make you better, you need to start by recognizing the importance of correcting this shortcoming. There's nothing I like better than to have someone come up to me after a talk and say, "Dr. Rotella, what I found out today is that the real heroics in golf occur not on the final green in some tournament. It's when no one's paying attention. It's when the player keeps that daily commitment to himself to practice and get better." That's when I feel I've delivered my message effectively. Keeping commitments is that important, that fundamental to real talent.

After recognizing the importance of sustaining commitment, you must focus on how you think of yourself. If you're a law student and you don't think of yourself as law review material, it's a lot more difficult to sustain the commitment to study every night. If you're a carpenter, and you don't see yourself as capable of building a fine house, it's nearly impossible to sustain the commitment to get out of bed early each morning and work on digging the foundation. You must begin to see yourself on the law review, to see the finished house. Once you do, sustaining the necessary commitment gets a lot easier.

This is why, I think, people who follow their dreams do better in the long run than people of great ability who either have no dreams or let others dream for them. The sports world is full of erstwhile young phenoms who fizzled as adults, either in sport or in later life. The reason, I think, is that they reached a point where they were no longer being pushed, prodded, and told what to do every day by a parent or coach. They reached a point where to keep getting better, they had to make and keep a commitment to themselves. And when they reached that point, they discovered they had no inner vision to help them sustain the commitment. In youth, they had relied on someone else's dream. In adulthood, people with lesser physical abilities but a sustaining dream kept their commitments and passed the phenoms by.

Commitment is nearly sacred to the most successful people I work with. They never merely go through the motions. They work with intensity. The strength of their commitments is such that they never let more than a day or two go by without following the regimen they know will lead to improvement and success. They catch themselves quickly when they start to fall away from their plan or their skills start to diminish. They don't let things slide till they're a week behind in their studies or they're hitting the ball sideways.

They almost welcome disappointment and adversity because they know that everyone faces some disappointment and adversity at some point. They know that their strong, committed response to setbacks is one of the things that will separate them from the mediocre masses. So they're enthused every day.

It never occurs to them that they might not attain their goals because their inner vision is so strong. You rarely hear them saying "I'll try" or "I hope I can" in reference to their commitments. They tend to say "I will."

Such commitment, harnessed to a dream, can produce magnificent achievement. Certainly it did for Pat Browne.

Pat has won the U.S. Blind Golfers' Association national championship twenty-one times, the last twenty consecutively, playing with Gerry Barousse as his coach. That's a record that I suspect will never be matched in any sport.

But his golf is not just good enough to win competitions for the blind. It's good enough to beat the overwhelming majority of sighted golfers. In his prime, in 1980, Pat played four consecutive rounds prior to the Braille Classic tournament at Mission Hills in Palm Springs, the site of the LPGA's Dinah Shore Invitational. He played those four rounds, from the middle tees, in 75, 74, 79, and 75.

Pat recalls very well the feeling he had when he finished that stretch of four rounds in the 70s. "I was ecstatic," he says. "I thought of all the loyal friends who'd helped me, and of all the distance I had come."

He had come, in fact, all the way back to the level of golf he was playing before his accident, when he had his sight.

He had shown us all what a person can achieve if he makes a commitment and sustains it with a vision.

CHAPTER SEVEN

There Is No Such Thing as Overconfidence

One of the most successful businesswomen of our time is Mary Kay Ash, founder of Mary Kay Cosmetics. She built a home-based business that sold a face cream into a multimillion-dollar, international beauty products enterprise.

I'm not qualified to judge the quality of her cosmetics, though I assume they're good. It's essentially irrelevant, because I know that it wasn't the quality of the cream that was the key to Mary Kay's success.

The key, I think, lies in a brooch that Mary Kay and her associates wear. It's a bumblebee. The bumblebee is a very important, symbolic totem for Mary Kay. As she explains it, "Aerodynamic engineers found out a long time ago that the bumblebee cannot fly. Its wings are too weak and its body is too heavy. But, fortunately, the bumblebee doesn't know that and it goes right on flying."

You can smile at this if you like and dismiss it as schmaltz.

But you do so at your peril, because that bumblebee brooch signifies something very important about real talent:

People with real talent believe they can accomplish anything they set their minds to until proven otherwise. People with real talent have confidence.

Mary Kay Ash understands this. When she founded her business, back in 1963, she understood that America had legions of women, most of them housewives, who had great energy and ability. She understood that many of them were failing to make full use of that ability and energy because they lacked confidence. They didn't believe in themselves. They did not know they could be successful. She recognized the potential for a business that could unleash their energy and ability by giving them a belief in themselves. She created such a business. She got thousands of women to dream.

And that, more than the quality of the creams and powders, is why Mary Kay has become a huge success. She understood the importance of creating confidence.

She came by her own confidence as the ironic result of a poor childhood. Mary Kay grew up in Texas, the child of an invalid father and a mother who had to work. Because she had no choice, Mary Kay's mother had to make her daughter confident and self-sufficient. From the age of eight or so, Mary Kay had to shop for groceries, cook meals, and ride the streetcars. Her mother guided her by telephone. Her slogan was, "You can do it, honey!"

Mary Kay drew often on the confidence her mother instilled in her. She married and had three children, but her husband came home from World War II and asked for a divorce. She had to find a way to support herself and her family. She went to work for a company called Stanley Home Products. Because of her confidence, she was a fine salesperson. She thrived on the company's internal competitions.

But as the years went by, she noticed that her company was willing to let a woman rise only to a certain level. She realized this after several men whom she'd trained became her supervisors. When she complained, she was told, "Well, the men have families to support." She pointed out that she, too, was supporting a family. It didn't help.

Her response, rather than getting discouraged, was to use her own confidence and her knowledge of its importance to found a company in which women would have no limits on how much they earned and how high they rose. Everything she has done with Mary Kay Cosmetics has emphasized the importance of instilling confidence in the women who sell its products. The results speak for themselves.

In any endeavor I've ever studied, from playing golf to selling lipstick, confidence is the single most important and least understood factor.

Without confidence, an individual is like an airplane without wings. No matter how powerful the engines are, the wingless airplane is not going to get off the ground. If you lack confidence, you're probably going to be nervous, tight, and hesitant in anything you try. You won't even try some things you could have succeeded at. And your preparation for performance is likely to be halfhearted. Why practice hard if you don't think you're going to succeed in the end?

If you don't prepare, if you perform hesitantly and if you give up easily, you can't expect to succeed. But that's the way people who lack confidence operate.

Such people probably believe, mistakenly, that confidence can only come from a history of successes. They say they're only being realistic if they lack confidence. *Unwittingly, they use "realism" as a justification for thinking negatively and limiting themselves.* How can they believe they can accomplish something if they've never done it before? Particularly if they've tried and failed in the past?

The answer goes back to free will. Confidence is nothing more than what you think about yourself in relation to a given challenge. It's not about where you've been. It's about where you're going. It's not about what you've done. It's about what you perceive you will do. You can choose what you think about yourself. People with real talent choose to think they can succeed. They prepare themselves to succeed.

Take, for example, my friend Davis Love III, the winner of the 1997 PGA Championship. If past performance were the only basis for confidence, Davis would have had to believe that he could never win the PGA. After all, he'd never won a major. Until 1995, he'd never even played particularly well in one.

And the 1997 PGA was played on a ferociously tough golf course, Winged Foot. With high rough, encroaching trees, and deep bunkers, Winged Foot punishes anyone who hits the ball off line. Once you're on the greens, the putts are fast and slippery. Very few people figured it to be the kind of course that favored Davis, who's a long hitter. He himself thought that the major he was most likely to win first was the Masters, because Augusta National rewards length.

Davis and I talked before the tournament. I reminded him that on a course like Winged Foot, in a major championship, not many players have the confidence required to win. A lot of them are intimidated right away. They go to the first tee on Thursday thinking, "I've never won a major and I've never played a course this tough. I just don't want to shoot in the 80s and look foolish." Others get to the first tee hoping they'll play well. But as soon as they hit a few balls into the rough, or three-putt on those slick greens, they, too, start thinking, "I just don't want to shoot in the 80s and look foolish."

These are the "realists." These are the ones who let experience dictate the level of their confidence.

To win, Davis would have to forget the fact that he'd never won a major. He'd have to shrug off the inevitable mistakes and the penalties they would exact. He'd have to find a way to keep thinking, "I can handle this course and win this tournament." He would, in a sense, have to defy experience.

I knew that Davis was ready to do this when our pre-tournament conversation turned to his putting. "We don't have to worry about that," he told me. "My routine is right on target. My putting is there."

What Davis meant was that he was not only setting himself up properly for each putt in the physical sense but he was also getting himself into the right frame of mind for each putt. He was stroking each one with the full intention of putting the ball in the hole. That was all he was thinking about as he putted.

That kind of confident attitude is essential to good putting. It means that each putt will be stroked instinctively and decisively. Does it mean that each putt will go in? Of course not. It simply means that the golfer will give himself the best possible chance to make each putt. You can't win a major championship without doing that.

That attitude extended to all the other clubs in Davis's bag. When he stood on the tees at Winged Foot and took his practice swings, he wasn't thinking about the bunkers or the rough. He was seeing the shot he wanted to play, the shape it would take, the place it would land.

He didn't let his attitude depend on whether putts dropped or drives hit fairways. He vowed to think the same way regardless of what happened to a given shot. He decided he could and would control his confidence.

That confidence, his trust that he could win, was critical in his ability to stay focused on one shot at a time. When you lack confidence, it's easy to get distracted by thoughts of mistakes that have happened or might happen. When you're confident, you remain composed. It's much easier to keep your mind in the present, where it must be. The same is true in a sales transaction, a meeting with a new client, or any business task.

Davis was confident—not because he had never missed key putts nor sprayed his tee shots in a major championship. He had. He was thinking confidently in spite of that history.

His confidence, then, was not the result of experience so much as it was the product of his will and his preparation. Davis made a conscious decision to follow a routine that included thinking only of the way he wanted his shots to fly and roll. He prepared diligently. He trained himself to execute those shots. So he could be confident even though he'd never won a major.

And that's the fundamental fact about confidence that so many people fail to grasp. It is the product not of experienced success, but of will and preparation.

~

Each of us has a jumble of different thoughts swirling about as we think of a particular challenge that faces us. Take a lawyer who's about to try a case. Her thoughts might fall into two categories. In Category A would be thoughts like, "I'm so pleased that my client selected me for this case. It shows that all the work I've done to improve my professional abilities is paying off. And I know exactly how to prepare for this case. I know the precedents to cite. I know how to discover the evidence. I know the witnesses we need and I know how to take their depositions. I suspect the other side is going to want to settle, and I'm sure I know just how to get as much as possible from a settlement negotiation. If we go to trial, they'll be sorry. I will outwork and outargue the other guys. I'll devise strategies to counter everything they can think of. I'll impress the jury, and in the end they'll wish they had settled."

In Category B, our lawyer might have thoughts like, "I've never won a case this big. I'm in over my head. I always blow big opportunities like this. The other side's lawyers are probably going to pull some tricky move that will sway the jury no matter how sound my case is. I never get any luck with juries. I don't think they like the way I look."

To put things very simply, confident people, people with real talent, find ways to allow thoughts from Category A to dominate their thinking. People who lack confidence and don't know how to develop it tend to let thoughts from Category B dominate.

You may object that you can't select the thoughts that come to your mind. And it is true that even the most confident person is occasionally plagued by irrational doubts. But your thoughts are like people that knock on the front door of your house. You can't control who walks up and knocks. You can control which ones you let in and entertain as guests.

The first step in taking control of your thoughts is to monitor them. Most of us aren't acutely aware of the thoughts that occupy our mind. They're too familiar to us. They become like the houses and buildings along the roads we drive every day on our way to and from work. We don't notice them.

When you begin to make an effort to monitor your thinking, you will notice these thoughts. It helps in this process to do something tangible, particularly when you notice a negative thought of the type from the lawyer's Category B. Some people write down their thoughts. Some people get a counter, keep it in a pocket and click it every time they notice a negative thought. Some use little devices like paper clips that they transfer from one pocket to another each time something negative occurs to them.

If you try this, you will probably notice that you have more negative thoughts than you expected. Most people, if asked, describe themselves as positive thinkers, even if they're the types of people who continually talk themselves into depression, lassitude, and defeat.

But as you continue with the monitoring process, you'll also probably notice a few immediate benefits. One is that when you monitor your negative thoughts, you hold them up to the light of scrutiny. And under scrutiny, many of them start to seem very dubious and irrational.

Take, for instance, our lawyer. Suppose she catches herself thinking, "I always blow big opportunities like this."

Under scrutiny, the foolishness of this thought is evident. She's been lying to herself in a negative way. If she always blew big opportunities, she would never have finished college and qualified for law school. She would never have gotten through her job interview and been hired by her firm. She would never have racked up all the achievements and successes in her life.

Upon reflection, our lawyer might well amend this unfounded, negative thought to something more realistic like, "I've been able to take advantage of opportunities when I worked hard and prepared intelligently. I've blown some when I was lax in my work and preparation. If I want to take advantage of this opportunity, I need to work hard and work smart."

People with real talent have this facility. They catch their negative thoughts and turn them into something realistic and positive. *In fact, I don't often use the term "positive thinking." I like the term "honest thinking," because that's what confidence really is.*

The more people think honest, positive thoughts, the more accustomed they become to it. Confidence becomes a habit. You can verify this if you use one of the techniques for monitoring your thoughts. After a while, you'll find that the number of times you write down a negative thought or transfer a paper clip greatly diminishes. You will have changed your way of thinking. And that means that you will have developed confidence.

111

Sometimes a client who has trouble with lack of confidence will listen to this and respond, "But that's not me, Doc. I'm not the kind of person who can go around all day imitiating the Little Engine That Could. I'm a little too cynical for that positive thinking stuff."

If that's your personal style, fine. *I don't ask that you walk around all day telling yourself what a swell, capable person you are. All I ask is that you eliminate the negative thoughts.*

If our lawyer, for instance, eliminates thoughts like "No matter what I do, they'll come up with some trick that will win the jury over," what is she left with? She's left with thoughts about how best to plan and prepare and argue the case in front of her.

She's left, in other words, thinking more or less the same way a confident person thinks. Confidence isn't some elixir. Remember that confidence is nothing more than the sum of the thoughts you have about yourself in relation to a particular challenge. If you're thinking about ways to overcome your challenge, you're thinking confidently.

A big part of this has to do with what you choose to remember. Do you dwell on your mistakes rather than learn from them and forget them? People with real talent develop a selective amnesia about their past. They have a long-term memory for success. They have a short-term memory for failure. They understand the truth of Mark Twain's remark that "The inability to forget is infinitely more devastating than the inability to remember."

❦

Don't confuse being confident with being Pollyanna, the fictional character who believed everything would turn out well no matter what she did or didn't do. You wouldn't want Pollyanna for a lawyer and you wouldn't want her flying your airliner in a winter storm. Confidence is not thinking, "I just know that somehow things will turn out all right." It's thinking, "I know that if I do all the things necessary to succeed, I will succeed."

Confident people are not free of worry. The most confident golfers I know, in fact, anticipate all the things that could go wrong in a round of golf—bad weather, slow play, bumpy greens, their own bad shots. Then they separate these worries into two categories—those they can do something about and those they can't. If it's something they can do something about, they do it. They practice bunker shots or pitches from dirt lies or whatever the weaknesses in their game might be. They pack extra towels and gloves and learn to keep them dry in the rain, so they're prepared for bad weather. If their worry is about something they can't control, like slow play in the group ahead of them, they resolve not to let the problem bother them. They mentally rehearse being unfazed. They rehearse the best possible responses to the situation, happy in

113

the knowledge that slow play, if it arises, will in fact work to their advantage, because they'll cope with it better than most of their competitors will.

In much the same way, a confident businesswoman anticipates problems and obstacles and plans her response to them. That's one way she remains confident.

People with real talent understand the importance of remaining confident. They monitor their thoughts and discipline themselves to resume thinking confidently whenever they find that their minds are wandering into doubt, fear, or self-pity.

I'm not trying to peddle the notion that confidence alone assures success. No matter how confidently I was thinking, I couldn't have won the PGA title that Davis Love III won last summer. Confidence has to be backed by skills. But skills also must be backed by confidence.

I often see skilled people fail precisely because they lack confidence. Especially in the early years of their careers, they worry so much about whether they can make the grade that they lose their focus and don't perform as well as they could if they understood the nature of confidence and how to develop it. Sometimes older workers develop a different variety of this problem. They let thoughts of past failures gradually overwhelm them. They're less confident at sixty than they were at forty. I tell people that with every passing year, with every increment of knowledge and experience, they should feel more confident, rather than less. If they don't, they're learning all the wrong things from their experience.

Sometimes, people who ordinarily have confidence lose it in intensified competition. They choose to focus not on their own performance but on the belief, whether right or wrong, that a competitor is better. This kind of belief becomes a self-fulfilling prophecy. Their own performance suffers because they don't believe in themselves. Their competitor wins, not necessarily because he's superior, but because he played his normal game and they didn't. If you're confident, you take care of your own performance, make it the best it can be, and let the results take care of themselves. If you don't win a particular game or sale or trial, you pick up and go on, knowing that next time might be different.

It's important to believe that in a competitive situation, where you've prepared properly, that you deserve success, that you're destined to attain it. That's the way people with real talent think.

❧

The questions I get when I lecture or appear on a radio call-in show suggest that a lot of people don't understand this. I see a world where people routinely cripple themselves because of lack of confidence. I see a world where people with fine skills postpone taking on challenges and pursuing their dreams because they tell themselves they're not ready yet. Yet I'm almost always asked not about the lack of confidence but about the dangers of overconfidence. People want to know how I cope with all the big egos I work with, as if there were something inherently wrong with having a big ego. People love to hear success stories, but for some reason they tend not to like people who are highly successful. They express this dislike by asking about overconfidence.

My answer is that there is no such thing as overconfidence.

I like working with big egos, because a big ego implies that an individual can see himself accomplishing big things. If he can, that makes my job easier.

I often have to remind athletes to be wary of the usual public reaction to healthy confidence. People tend to label healthy confidence as overconfidence. If an athlete listens to them, he can start to doubt his own good attitude. He can adopt an inappropriate humility that undermines his skills. He can become the kind of kid who costs his team a game because he won't take the open shot with seconds left to play, thinking that the crowd would consider him immodest for wanting that shot.

To be sure, I've seen cases of false confidence. There are indeed people who lack skills and competence, who fail to prepare, and who then try to put up a positive facade. They mouth confident platitudes to justify their laziness. There are runners who don't train but go to the starting line telling their competition they're going to blow their doors off. There are salespeople who don't prepare for sales meetings but walk in with a swagger and a big smile. There are students who don't bother to study for exams but tell their friends they're going to pull an A.

Such people, once the time comes to perform, generally can't maintain their facades. They start to sweat. They tighten up. They choke. Because they know, deep inside, that they haven't prepared themselves. They have no reason to feel confident.

And I've seen cases of arrogance. There are, unfortunately, athletes and performers in every field who mistakenly think that their skill and success somehow make them bigger, better, and more important than mere mortals. They haven't learned to rein their confidence in once they step off the course or out of the courtroom. They're obnoxious to the people around them.

But I've never seen someone who's put in the time and the work to attain competence who then ruins his performance by being overconfident. The more confidence a performer has during a performance, the better he is likely to perform.

Consider, for example, a concert pianist. Let's assume he is not falsely confident. He's not lazy. He has put in the time and practice to master the piece of music he's going to play. He respects its difficulty, but he knows he has the skills he needs to play it. He follows a routine that he has devised to bring his body and mind to a peak when he walks out on stage. He is confident.

Is there any way he can be overconfident in his performance? No. The more confident he is, the more he can let the music flow from within himself, the more he can show people his artistry, his mastery. The more confident he is, the better he plays. His real talent and his musical talent mesh and harmonize.

If you want to develop real talent you must realize the importance of confidence. Your brain operates in some respects like a computer. The quality of the data the computer spits out depends directly on the quality of the data that you put in. Your thoughts about yourself are the data you input. If they're heavily negative, the brain will respond to that and produce a corresponding performance.

It's fairly easy to think confidently when things are going well. You just go with the flow of your perceptions. It's when things get tough, as they invariably do, that people with real talent separate themselves from the competition by finding ways to think confidently despite the hard times.

It's in times of adversity that you most need confidence. You may think that you're trying hard to overcome difficult circumstances. But if you lack confidence, you're like someone trying to dig a hole with a thimble. Yes, you're working hard, but you're not going to beat someone with a shovel.

Study after study has shown this. Insurance companies that hire thousands of new agents have found that academic records and test scores are not nearly as helpful in predicting which ones will succeed as is an accurate assessment of a person's tendency to be confident and optimistic. People with confident, optimistic outlooks tend to succeed. People who are pessimistic, who lack confidence, tend to fail. Yet, most companies don't train their employees in confidence, or don't devote nearly as much time and effort to it as they do to teaching something like computer skills. That's because computer skills are tangible and measureable. Confidence happens to be neither.

It also happens to be more important.

The good news about confidence is that you get to choose whether you're going to have it. Some people have to work at it harder than others, but confidence is a skill like any other. It can be learned and it must be practiced. I sometimes ask people what they would do if they found themselves in a situation where the lack of a single skill was blocking them from success. Suppose that to be a great marketer, you needed to learn how to handle statistics. Would you learn statistics? Or would you give up and moan about your bad luck?

Obviously, if you wanted to succeed, you'd learn statistics. It's the same way with confidence. If you want it you can have it. If you want to succeed, you'll learn to be confident.

CHAPTER EIGHT

How Real Talent Responds to Failure

Henry Ford was a failure. Around the turn of the century he founded a company called the Detroit Automobile Co. It didn't make money and the stockholders forced him to resign. The company was reorganized and changed its name to Cadillac.

Sam Walton was a failure. When he got out of the Army after World War II, he borrowed $25,000 from his father-in-law and bought a five-and-dime franchise in Newport, Arkansas. He lost the store after five years because he'd signed a lease that didn't give him an option to renew. He had to leave town.

Berry Gordy was a failure. In 1953, just back from a stint with the Army in Korea, he opened a record store in his native Detroit. It specialized in the music he loved, jazz. But the neighborhood liked blues and his store failed. Gordy tried songwriting. No one liked his songs. In fact, people laughed at them. His in-laws finally got him a job on an automobile assembly line.

Bill Gates and Paul Allen were failures. They graduated from high school with a passion for computers. They founded a company called Traf-O-Data to sell software that would help municipal traffic and road departments count the cars that passed given points each day. Traf-O-Data never made money and it folded some years later.

Lee Iacocca was a failure. Early in his tenure at Ford Motor Co., the carmaker had some staff cutbacks and Iacocca was demoted. He persisted, won his old job back, and eventually became president of the company. But he failed in the most significant task for a Ford executive in those days, which was staying on the good side of Henry Ford II. Ford fired him. The worst part was that many of the Ford executives Iacocca had thought were his friends stopped talking to him.

Wally Amos was a failure. He trained for a job in the restaurant business at New York City's Food Trades Vocational High School. The school helped arrange his first job, at the Essex House Hotel in New York, working in the pantry. Amos wanted to move up to a job behind the range, preparing entrées in the hotel's restaurant. But after a while, he noticed that only white students were moved into those jobs. He was black. Discouraged, he gave up on being a cook and joined the Air Force.

If you know anything about American business, of course, you know that Henry Ford, Sam Walton, Berry Gordy, Bill Gates, Paul Allen, Lee Iacocca, and Wally Amos didn't remain failures. Henry Ford went on to found the company that bears his name. Berry Gordy started Motown Records. Bill Gates and Paul Allen founded Microsoft. Wally Amos created Famous Amos chocolate chip cookies. Lee Iacocca rescued Chrysler. They all became major success stories. They all were people with real talent.

I've recounted their inauspicious moments because they illustrate an extremely important fact about real talent. *People with real talent fail, just as do people without real talent. What sets them apart is the way they respond to failure.*

When they fail, people with real talent don't permit themselves to entertain cosmic, debilitating thoughts like "I'm no good. I just don't have it. I'll never be any good."

Nor do they blame their failure on someone or something else. They look honestly at what happened and their own shortcomings. But they focus on things that are temporary and remediable rather than things that are beyond their control. They see failure as a temporary setback rather than a life sentence.

Sam Walton responded to his failure with his first five-and-dime store by chastising himself for lack of foresight in the way he negotiated his lease. He resolved never to allow that to happen again. He moved to Bentonville, Arkansas, and opened a store he called Wal-Mart. And then he did one of the things people with real talent generally do in the face of failure.

He resolved that if he failed again, it was not going to be because one of his competitors outworked him. No merchant in Arkansas put in longer hours than Sam Walton.

He capitalized on what he had learned from his first venture. In many respects, his first store had done well. That experience had proven several things to Sam Walton. One was that if you looked hard enough, you could find ways to buy merchandise for less. Two was that people would respond to stores that offered real bargains. And the third thing was that a lot of retailers had gotten fat and comfortable on a system of little real competition and big markups. To make sure he was never as vulnerable again to what happened with one piece of property, he spread his stores around to different small towns.

He was in many respects a driven man. There was not much he wouldn't do to cut his company's costs and undercut the competition's prices. When he and his staff went to New York to buy merchandise in the early days, they often slept seven or eight to a hotel room. That was not such a hardship, since they were rarely in the room. They were working too hard.

If you've driven around the United States, you already have a fair idea of the rest of the story. Wal-Mart became an enormous retail chain. By the end of his life, Sam Walton was, by some reckonings, the wealthiest man in America. Toward the end, he was asked what had made him successful.

He had a list of smart ideas for retailers. But the first thing he said was, "Friend, we just got after it and stayed after it."

That's a fair summation of one of the first things that people with real talent do in response to failure. They get after it and they stay after it.

When I counsel salespeople, that's the first thing I bring up if they want some advice on how to respond to failure. Let's make sure no one is outworking you. Once we're sure you're working harder than anyone else, we'll look at other things if you're not yet as successful as you want to be.

There's a bit of a myth in this country that people are working too hard. The media tell us that because they've learned that we like to read it about ourselves. I realize that people have a lot of demands on their time, especially in households where both spouses are trying to pursue careers and raise children at the same time. But if you followed people in the normal office around for a day, you'd be amazed at how much time they waste. We do have our workaholics, but we have a lot more people who aren't putting full effort into their jobs during the time they're at work.

Avoiding stress is often used as an excuse for not working hard. When I finished graduate school, stress reduction and stress management were very fashionable. In fact, I taught a course in stress reduction techniques for several years. But the more I observed people who found ways to succeed and people who found ways to fail, the more convinced I became that stress reduction and stress management have little or nothing to do with either excellence or happiness.

The most successful, happiest people I know thrive on what many would consider stress. That's because they perceive stressful situations not as threats or burdens but as challenges they can overcome. They have a certain hardiness.

People who fall short of their dreams and potential often use stress and the avoidance of stress as a rationalization for failure. They don't understand that the worst kind of stress comes from the unavoidable realization that you're wasting your life.

That's not to say that everyone doesn't need recreation and an occasional break from work. Everyone does. And it's not to say that you don't need to strive to be calm and calculating, as opposed to tense and irritable, in the face of stress. You do.

But I believe that the human organism was designed to be usefully aroused and engaged by stressful situations. People with real talent understand this. When they're under stress, they use it as extra motivation for the kind of smart, hard work that will lead to success.

In fact, if you look around your company for the person who's working hardest and smartest, and you match or exceed his or her effort, I guarantee you that no matter how skilled you are, or what other problems you have, you're going to do well and you will be happier. Working hard is not always the whole answer to failure, but it's usually a big part of the answer. If you work hard, you're usually going to do well.

Yet most people respond to failure in exactly the opposite way. They work less rather than more. Why? The key lies in the way they perceive their failures. They find certain kinds of rationalizations:

"I'm not talented enough."

"The boss doesn't want me to succeed because I'm not his favorite."

"This job is just too hard. No one could do well at it."

These rationalizations have two debilitating things in common. One, they take the responsibility out of the rationalizer's hands. If you're not good enough, or the boss is against you, or the job is just too hard, then failure obviously isn't your fault, right? You did everything you could. But the deck was stacked against you. And two, you can't do anything about it. You can't change your God-given talent, change your boss, or change the nature of the job you're assigned. You're helpless. Everything is beyond your control.

In such circumstances, why work harder? You've given yourself an excuse to give up. You have talked yourself into being helpless.

People with real talent perceive their failures differently. They attribute them to factors they can change and control. They tell themselves things like:

"I didn't make the sale, but that wasn't a rejection of me

personally. I'll keep trying, and when they get to know me, they'll buy. And that will be a reflection on me."

"I failed, but I didn't give it my best effort. If I work hard enough, I think I can succeed."

"I failed, but I take pride in being a professional. That means I'm not going to let that failure affect the next call I make. It will be just as good as the last one."

"I made the best presentation possible, but it didn't work out. The next time it probably will."

"I worked hard, but I didn't work smart enough. I'm going to get someone to help me with my presentation skills and figure out ways to be more persuasive. At least I've learned what doesn't work."

"I failed, but that just puts me one step closer to my goal. So it's progress."

If the last statement sounds impossibly optimistic to you, remember the case of Bob Sherman, who now manages the eastern United States for Merrill Lynch. In his business, as in many sales businesses, the failure rate is quite high. Bob figured that twenty-four out of twenty-five prospects would turn him down. He didn't let those rejections bother him as long as he knew he was working hard and honing his sales skills. He figured that every prospect who turned him down was an accomplishment because the rejection put him that much closer to the prospect who would say yes.

This is the way people with real talent choose to perceive their failures. In a seminar I once taught at the University of

Virginia, I had a student-athlete named Stuart Anderson. He played football for the Cavaliers and went on to the National Football League after he graduated.

The group was discussing confidence in athletics when Stuart told a story from his high school days. He played basketball as well as football in high school, and in his senior year, his team advanced to the state playoffs. "I was," Stuart told the class, "a 50 percent shooter from the floor."

But in the first round of the playoffs, Stuart started badly. His first shot missed. He took another shot. It missed. He missed about twenty shots in a row. But Stuart didn't let those misses bother him. In fact, he figured that each miss only increased the likelihood that the next shot would go in. He was, after all, a 50 percent shooter.

This dumbfounded some of the other students in the class. How could he think that way, they asked. If he missed twenty in a row, didn't it mean he was having an off night? Should he have started passing the ball to other players instead of taking shots?

"No," Stuart replied. "Because I'm a shooter."

The game came down to the wire, with Stuart's team trailing by a point. They got the ball with a few seconds left and called time out. The coach, figuring that Stuart was in a slump, diagrammed a play that put the ball into the hands of a junior for the final shot.

"Wait a minute, Coach!" Stuart objected. "I want that shot."

The other kid didn't really want the pressure of the final shot, so the coach acceded and called a play for Stuart.

The seconds ticked down, they got the ball to Stuart, and he turned and shot.

Nothing but net.

His teammates and the fans carried him off the floor, Stuart recalled with satisfaction. His picture was in all the papers the next day. But Stuart didn't think the shot was so surprising. He just figured he was way overdue.

"Suppose," one kid asked him, "that you had hit your first five shots in a row. Would you have thought that you were due to miss some?"

"Of course not," Stuart replied. "Then I'd figure I was on a hot streak and they couldn't stop me."

Stuart, one could say, understood the true nature of failure. Taking the shot and missing it is not failure. Failure is letting fear prevent you from taking the shot at all. Failure is letting fear prevent you from making the next call or trying for the next promotion.

Most people never understand this. They can't get around the sting of an initial setback. Maybe they get to college with dreams of becoming a physician. They make a C in their first semester of chemistry. It's a crushing disappointment.

Rather than face the possibility of that kind of pain again, they drop chemistry. They forget all about the good grades they had in high school science. They don't consider the possibility that they need some new study skills to keep up and excel in a competitive university. They don't consider the possibility of working harder. They think only of the humiliation and embarrassment they felt when their friends and family found out that they couldn't cut it in their first college-level chemistry course.

They find it a whole lot easier to switch to geology and decide that they're going to get a dull, safe job in an office somewhere than to stick it out, try harder, and expose themselves to another possible failure.

I see this same tendency in the consulting work I do. Once in a while, a supervisor and I will meet with a sales rep who the supervisor thinks could be a brilliant success. This might be a man or a woman who is cruising along with $200,000 in annual commissions. That's certainly enough to be comfortable but it's not enough to be a star.

"You could be a million-dollar producer," the boss tells this person.

You might think that the sales rep would be thrilled to hear this vote of confidence in his ability. The opposite is usually the case. The man's brow furrows. He frowns. He squirms in his chair. Because he really doesn't want to hear that.

He'd much rather continue in his comfortable, pressureless, slightly above average rut than face a challenge to improve his performance, even though improving his performance will mean more money for him and his family.

The fact is that if he decides to try for a million-dollar year, he might not make it. He's afraid to put himself in a situation where he's got some risk of failing. He'd rather preserve the illusion of being successful than risk failure to find out how good he can be.

What a contrast this is to the way we were as kids! When I speak with parents, or with high school students, I so often hear about kids who are frustrated and unhappy because the coach won't give them a chance to shine. They pray for a chance to play. They pray that the coach will notice them, have faith in them. They'd give anything to be the one the coach turns to for the last shot with the game on the line. That's their dream.

But as adults, too many people have traded their dreams and aspirations for safety and the illusion of security. They're doing everything they can to avoid exposing themselves to the risk of failure. If the boss calls them into the office and tells them he wants them to star, to lead the team, to perform on a higher level, they respond with inward indignation. "I know why you're telling me I have talent. You're trying to put pressure on me! You're trying to manipulate me," they think. "After you tell me how good I could be, then you're going to tell me if I don't measure up, I'm a bad person or I'm a failure."

If they were still playing basketball, they'd be aspiring to the job of twelfth man on the Chicago Bulls, because what they'd really like is to sit, watch, and let Michael Jordan win championship rings and bonus checks for them.

When I was a graduate student at the University of Connecticut, I assisted the coach of the lacrosse team. I was young and enthusiastic. I had the squad do autumn conditioning work. I held practice late on winter evenings at a local high school gym. I expected a lot from the kids on the team and they responded. In my first season working with them, the team went something like 8-3.

After that season was over, the coach of another sport at Connecticut invited me to lunch. I was glad to go, because I've always liked picking the brains of coaches. But what I heard from this guy made me lose my appetite quickly.

"You've done a fine job with that lacrosse team, Bob," he said. "Lots of pep, lots of enthusiasm. But, you know, I've been coaching for a while, and it's my experience that it's best to have teams that break even, that win about half their games."

I was dumbfounded. I scratched my head.

"If you keep winning eight or nine games a year," he explained, "people are going to start to expect that. Then if you have a season or two where you only win half your games, they're going to figure you're slacking off and maybe they better find a new coach. But if you always win about half your games, no one's going to get angry and no one's going to have high expectations. You're safe."

I didn't tell this coach what I thought of his ideas. Sadly, through the years, I've found that he is not alone. There are many coaches out there who look for a safe niche. They don't do what it takes to be great because they don't want the risks involved, the risk of failure. When they recruit, they don't go after the superlative athletes, because they don't want some newspaper writing that the kid chose College X over their school. They recruit kids they know they can get. They aim for a spot just above mediocrity. The kids, sensing this, perform accordingly.

The greats have conquered this fear of failure. When I worked with the Chicago Cubs, I got to know Greg Maddux, who is without doubt the outstanding pitcher of this decade. In pitching, there are several points where pitchers face fear. One is the first pitch to every batter. They have to be willing to throw a strike most of the time. They have to be willing to face the possibility that the hitter is going to knock it out of the ballpark. And there are three innings in particular when a pitcher tends to be fearful. One is the first, when he's finding out how well he's throwing on a given day. Another is the fifth, when he's striving to become the pitcher of record, to pitch the minimum number of innings required to earn a win. And the last is the ninth, when shutouts and complete games are on the line. Most pitchers tend to get tight and careful in those situations. Greg pitches without fear. That's one big reason why he's been so successful with an 87-miles-per-hour fastball—that and the fact that he realizes that the velocity of a pitcher's fastball isn't as important as the contrast between his fastball and his off-speed pitches. Greg wins by throwing an early strike or two, getting hitters behind in the count, and then destroying their timing with his changes of speed. He is fearless.

I used to tell pitchers on the Cubs, "Let's pretend we're playing catch with the catcher. Let's not think differently if there's a heavy hitter at the plate. Let's be in control of our minds."

Greg responded, "I do that on every pitch."

He reminds me of something I heard about Ted Williams of the Boston Red Sox. In the 1941 season, Williams hit brilliantly. The Yankees, though, had a better all-around lineup and by the last weekend of the season, they had clinched the American League pennant. After the Red Sox' game on Saturday, the next-to-last day of the season, Williams was hitting .3996. Since averages are rounded off, this meant he was hitting .400 for the season, a rare feat that had not been accomplished since Bill Terry of the New York Giants hit .401 in 1930.

"Congratulations, Ted," the sportswriters said after the game. "You've hit .400."

"Wait a minute," Williams said. "The season's not over. We've got a doubleheader tomorrow."

"Those games don't mean anything, Ted," the writers responded. "You're going to sit them out, aren't you? Don't you want to protect this average?"

No way, Williams said, though his actual language may have been saltier. "You guys don't get it. Tomorrow is going to be the most exciting day of my life, a day I've been dreaming about since I was a little kid. Tomorrow is when I get to find out if I'm a .400 hitter."

Williams played both games of the Red Sox doubleheader the next day. He made six hits. He finished the season with a batting average of .406, a standard that has not been matched in major league baseball for going on sixty years.

If Ted Williams had any fears of going hitless on the last day and losing his chance at a .400 average, he ignored them. That's what people with real talent do. They focus on their dreams, on what they want, rather than what they're afraid may happen if they fail. They go for greatness.

They understand that happiness comes not from success, and certainly not from avoiding failure. Happiness comes from being able to look at yourself in the mirror at the end of the day, or at the end of your life, and know that you took on the biggest challenge you could find and did your absolute best with it.

CHAPTER NINE

Following a Blazed Trail

For all of recorded history through the first half of this century, no human being ran a mile in less than four minutes. Many gifted runners competed in the mile, and they brought the world record down to the neighborhood of 4:01. But there progress stopped.

There was a certain symmetry to the idea of a mile in four minutes—four laps around a standard track, a minute per lap. It was an obvious target, a dream. But no one could do it. Eventually, "experts" came along who "proved" that human beings were physiologically incapable of a four-minute mile, that they just couldn't ingest and process oxygen fast enough to carry themselves that far, that fast. Sportswriters began talking of the four-minute "barrier" as if it were an insuperable physical object.

In the early 1950s, an accomplished British runner named Roger Bannister entered medical school. In part as a result of his studies, he decided that the experts were wrong. He calculated that a man could run a mile in less than four minutes, and he committed himself to doing it. On a drizzly day in the spring of 1954 he proved his point, breaking the world record with a time just a fraction of a second under four minutes. It was one of the athletic milestones of our time.

What's interesting to me is what happened after Bannister broke the barrier. Within a few years, a lot of milers were dipping under four minutes. Bannister's record was broken repeatedly. He didn't even win the 1,500 meters at the 1956 Olympics. By the 1960s, the mile record was approaching 3:50 and high school boys were breaking four minutes.

Roger Bannister had acted as a powerful role model. Once he showed that running a four-minute mile was possible, he inspired dozens of runners to intensify their commitments, train more rigorously, and improve their performances. Were these runners more talented than the generations of pre-Bannister milers who had never bettered four minutes? Were they genetically superior in some way? I don't think so. They just had a better role model.

Role models and mentors play an important part in the success of people with real talent. They can impart skills, either by example or by actively teaching us. More important, they can help us keep our commitments.

I've spoken about how people who keep commitments tend to do so not because they experience constant success and positive feedback, but because they never lose sight of what they are trying to become and they never lose the faith that they can achieve what they've set out to achieve. A role model reinforces your vision and your faith. By standing where you'd like to stand, he reminds you that it's possible to get there.

I certainly had my share of role models when I was growing up. The Boston Celtics were the pride of New England and players like Bob Cousy, Paul Silas, and John Havlicek set great examples for me. I watched very few Celtic games. They were rarely on television in those days. We used to listen to them on the radio. I can remember many hours shooting hoops outside my house with the radio in a propped-open window, listening to the Celtics. I think that the radio was a factor in making the Celtics great role models. With television, you tend to watch passively. With radio, your imagination is engaged as you envision what the players are doing. From there, it's a short step to envisioning yourself doing the same thing. I can remember trying to dribble like Cousy, trying to play defense like Havlicek, trying to box out and grab rebounds like Silas.

Interestingly enough, I wasn't much inspired by the greatest Celtic of that era, Bill Russell. It's because Russell was a big man, a foot taller than I was ever going to be. There wasn't much use in trying to imitate the way he blocked a shot under the basket, plucked the ball from the air and fired the outlet pass to start the Celtics' fast break. I wasn't going to do that. I concentrated on the Celtics whose skills and work habits I could hope to copy. I can still remember being impressed by an article Paul Silas wrote about the thought he put into offensive rebounding. He studied the characteristic misses of every Celtic shooter and set up accordingly. Anyone could copy that kind of diligence.

I had a similar kind of selectivity in picking role models from other teams and other sports. I used to be a bit of a heretic for a New Englander in those years. I rooted for the New York Yankees. But while I might try to imitate the way Billy Martin hustled at second base, I was never tempted to copy his carousing habits off the field.

When I was a boy, I idolized some of the best high school athletes in Rutland. I watched the way they practiced, the way they played. I tried to imitate them. But if, as sometimes happened, one of those high school stars went off to college and went astray, if he dropped out of school, got married, and started smoking cigarettes, I immediately forgot about him. I never gave a thought to the notion that I ought to do as my erstwhile hero had done. I just found a new role model who could help show me the way to where I wanted to go.

This is a trait I often see in people with real talent. They have a knack for picking and choosing the characteristics in their role models that will help them. They ignore the ones that won't. They tend to be less than infatuated with the precocious, natural talents that the rest of society lionizes. They realize that precocious talent is useless as a role model.

Tiger Woods, for example, has limited value as a role model for most golfers. He's a fine young man and he shows us how far a golf ball can be hit accurately. But he was hitting golf balls 300 yards when he was fourteen years old. Very few people have Tiger's physical gifts. They're wasting their time when they stand on the range trying to hit the ball as far as Tiger does. Tiger may someday be a useful model for how a champion works to stay at the top once he's gotten there. But for the time being, there isn't all that much we can learn from him about attitude.

People with real talent are far more likely to focus on someone like Tom Lehman and draw inspiration from the way Lehman never gave up on himself after he fell off the PGA Tour in 1984. They'll try to imitate the way Lehman kept working on his game and believing in himself through years of wandering in the mini-tour wilderness before finding great success in his late thirties. It takes nothing away from Tiger Woods to say that for most of us, Tom Lehman is a much more useful role model. People with real talent pick useful role models.

This is especially true of women and members of minority groups. As a white male, I can only deplore the discrimination that women and minorities still face as they try to succeed. It's a problem that society needs to work on and solve. But I can't agree when a woman or a minority member tells me, as some of them did in my classes at the University of Virginia, that they have no role models.

There are role models out there for everyone. Women and minorities just have to be a little more creative in finding them.

◆⌐○

I know a woman named Jennie Johnson who spent two years in Charlottesville a couple of decades ago when her husband, Dave, was studying for his master's degree in business administration.

Jennie was a determined and capable woman who had finished her bachelor's degree in three years. But she soon found that being determined and capable was not as important, in the eyes of many prospective employers, as the fact that she was a woman. The only job she could find in Charlottesville was as secretary to the headmaster at a private school. She got that job only because she pretended she knew how to take dictation. Actually, she only scribbled in her steno book when her boss dictated a letter. Then she wrote up what her boss wanted to say, polishing his language as she did so. He never caught on.

She realized that she wanted more from her career than secretarial work and faking dictation, so she got a master's degree from Virginia in public administration. She thought that the public sector might be more receptive to women than the private sector.

It wasn't. After her husband graduated, they moved to Winston-Salem, North Carolina, where he had been offered a banking job. Jennie called a local politician who was a friend of a friend. She explained that she had just gotten her master's degree in public administration and was hoping to land a position in government.

"I'm sorry," the politician said politely. "I don't know of any secretarial jobs open."

"Maybe I didn't make myself clear," Jennie said. "I have a master's degree in public administration."

"Oh," the politician replied. "Well, I don't know of anyone who's looking for an executive secretary, either."

This sort of attitude seemed primitive to Jennie, but she did her best to ignore it. "If you let it bother you, you quit," she says.

She worked for a health planning council for a while, then for the local United Way. She realized she was not likely to achieve her financial goals working for a nonprofit organization, but she understood that the job was valuable for the contacts she made in the Winston-Salem business community. Eventually she moved into a job on the planning staff at an insurance company called Integon.

The insurance business was not, at the time, rife with professional women. In fact it was one of the more male-dominated industries in the country. When Jennie looked up the ladder, she saw no women she could emulate. And she wasn't the sort of woman who could simply adopt the male culture as a way of making friends and getting ahead. She didn't, for example, play golf and she had no desire to learn.

So she studied the behavior of the bosses she had and tried to pick out what was effective and ineffective. She saw some men who struck her as smart, but arrogant. They used fear and intimidation to motivate their subordinates. This style got some superficial results. People came to work on time and did what they were told. But these managers got no input from their subordinates. They made mistakes they could have avoided if they had gotten more help and ideas from the people who worked for them. And eventually this caught up with them and they were fired.

Jennie also saw bosses who seemed to like to develop the talents of those who worked for them. They encouraged people to make decisions and promote their ideas. They allowed them to make mistakes without retribution—up to a point, of course. They didn't seek the spotlight for themselves. They were good listeners. They made it a point to meet a broad spectrum of people. They read widely. They had ambition, but it was an ambition that was not directed against anyone. They wanted to move the company forward.

Jennie emulated these traits, but she did it in her own way. For instance, she had noticed that the effective bosses made it a point to have a broad range of contacts. They may have done this, in part, by playing golf or joining clubs where women weren't welcome. Jennie adopted the tactic, but she adapted it to her own interests. She loves the arts, so she got active with the Winston-Salem Arts Council; eventually, she was its president. She volunteered for community projects through the

Chamber of Commerce. She accomplished the same thing as her male role models had, but in a different style.

It would be an oversimplification to say that this knack for picking out particular traits in role models and imitating them in her own style has been responsible for Jennie's rise in the insurance business. Jennie joined the industry at a time when financial instruments of all sorts were beginning a rapid evolution. She was smart enough to foresee some of the ways that this would affect the insurance business. She got her M.B.A. as a part-time student. She positioned herself well and she took advantage of the opportunities that came her way.

A dozen years ago, Liberty Corporation of Greenville, South Carolina, which owns a large insurance company, recruited her to work as its vice president in charge of planning. Since then, she's risen to president of Liberty Insurance Services. She's one of the highest-ranking female executives in the insurance business.

She still uses the same strategies she worked out for herself in Winston-Salem. She continues to be interested in the arts. (If you fly into the Greenville-Spartanburg airport, you might notice the gallery for local artists along the concourse between the gates and the baggage claim area. That's Jennie's idea.) She continues to learn selectively from the people around her.

As she rises in the corporate hierarchy, she says, she sees that "some people get better and some give up." She's alert to that possibility in the people she's been learning from. When she finds that one of her role models has himself stopped making progress, she is undeterred. She looks for someone else who can help her learn what she needs to know to get to the next rung.

I heard similar things recently when I met Rick Hunt. Rick is the vice president for electronic media at Columbia House. He happens to be black. He's also a golfer. He called me not long ago and said that he'd read *Golf Is Not a Game of Perfect* and he thought he could improve his game further if he could consult with me personally. As I generally do with a new client, I invited him to stay overnight in our guest room while we spent a couple of days discussing him and his game.

That wouldn't be necessary, Rick said. He'd be staying at his grandmother's house in Charlottesville. And that was the first I heard of Rick's family background. It turned out to be an interesting and instructive story.

Rick was born in Charlottesville back in the days when the South was still largely segregated. Among his forebears were some of the pillars of the local black community. His grandmother's brothers ran the first sanitary barber shop for black men in Charlottesville. And his grandmother, Maude Fleming, taught for more than forty years in the Charlottesville schools.

Rick's parents moved to Philadelphia when he was quite young, but he spent nearly all of his vacations with his grand-

145

parents in Charlottesville. That meant that his grandparents spent a lot of time with him and were in a position to be role models for him.

They were quite different, as he recalls. His grandfather, who worked for the C&O Railroad, had suffered the slights and indignities the South in those years could inflict on a black man. Rick has memories of his grandfather complaining, for instance, that he was never allowed to try on shoes in a shoe store. He had to take them as they came in the box, pay for them, and hope they felt good when he got them home and tried them on. His grandfather, Rick recalls, was a bitter man.

His grandmother, operating in much the same environment, responded differently. Rick recalls her as a short, strong, cheerful, and optimistic woman who always wore a hat and a dress when she went out. Mrs. Fleming knew that there were white-owned stores that treated blacks badly. She simply avoided them. She shopped at places where she was treated with respect. Rick can recall buying furniture with her and being impressed by the way the shopkeeper called her "Mrs. Fleming." His grandmother, he says, was a positive person.

Presented with two potential role models, both of whom he loved, Rick gravitated toward his grandmother. He sympathized with his grandfather, but he realized, perhaps just instinctively, that his grandmother's attitude toward the world would take him farther than his grandfather's.

His parents reinforced this attitude. From the first grade on, they sent him to a small Quaker school in Philadelphia, a school which, as Rick puts it, "was multiracial before it was hip to be multiracial." He recalls that it was several years before he and his white classmates realized there were racial differences between them. "We were never taught to hate," he recalls. "By the time we got old enough to realize we were different, we were a community."

When it came time for college, Rick and his parents and grandparents had already chosen a role model for him. His mother and grandmother were big supporters of President John F. Kennedy. From the time he was four or five, they had been telling him that he, too, ought to go to Harvard, Kennedy's alma mater. Rick applied and was admitted.

He was the first in his family to go to a predominantly white college. "Kennedy was a very big symbol and promise of hope for a future that they never had," he says of his mother and grandmother. "People bought into that."

Rick did well at Harvard, got a master's in management at Yale, and eventually went into the music business because he thought it would be a fine way to blend a lifelong interest in playing and performing with his interest in business. His grandmother is still, in many respects, a role model for him.

Like her, he is cheerful and optimistic. He expects people to treat him with respect and tries to deal with those who do so. Early in his career, he was offered a role managing marketing for black artists. He told his superiors he wanted to be considered for a job managing both black and white performers, and he pointed out that he had the background and experience to handle both. He got what he wanted.

It's not that he doesn't encounter racism. Rick has a voice that, as he says, doesn't "sound stereotypically black." Sometimes, dealing with someone who knows him only through telephone conversations, he'll hear something he knows he would not hear if he were talking face-to-face.

"Someone might say he's looking for a singing actress for a sitcom," he recounts. "And I'll suggest someone. And he'll say, 'How black is she?' because he doesn't want someone whose skin is too dark or whose mannerisms might strike a white audience as 'too black.' And a voice inside me screams, 'Oh, about as black as me.' But I don't say that. I just say I'll send him a picture.

"For one thing," Rick continues, "the experience of meeting that guy one day and seeing his reaction when he realizes I'm black is too rich to be missed."

For another, he has his grandmother's example of someone who refused to let racism poison her own attitude. "I live every hour of every day with the understanding that I'm an African-American," he says. "But I still believe that what happens to me is much more in my control than in anyone else's, and I'm not willing to give that up. If I were to give in to racism, to become bitter, it would mean I would not be able to stretch myself to my limits."

I'm pleased to say that Rick's golf scores improved after we worked together. His personal best for 18 holes dropped from 79 to 76. His handicap dropped from 12 to single digits.

He's kind enough to say that some of the things that we talked about help him in business as well as on the golf course. The notion of trusting your swing and "freeing it up" suggests to Rick that the creative side of his job requires him to be just as loose and just as trusting of his own skills and judgment. The idea that you have to have a long memory for your good shots and a short memory for your bad ones also resonates. "I tend to dwell on my failures," he says. "But I have a devil of a time telling you things I did right. I have to work on that."

I think he will work on it and I think he will have many more successes. But I'm dead certain that whatever Rick accomplishes will be a whole lot more attributable to the things he learned from his grandmother than to anything I told him.

The principles that Jennie Johnson and Rick Hunt applied in their search for role models apply to anyone, regardless of gender or race. *You will rarely, no matter what your field or where you work, find a role model who checks exactly the same boxes on the personnel form that you check. But you can almost always find someone who does a few things—perhaps no more than one or two—that you'd like to do.*

People with real talent cultivate a relationship with this

sort of person. Without being obsequious or annoying, they find ways to observe and chat with the person who's worth emulating. They separate the valuable characteristics from the ones that aren't helpful. And they incorporate what they learn into their own work.

CHAPTER TEN

The People Who Support You

I was dining not long ago at the home of Christy and Tom Kite in Austin. Tom, of course, is a long-standing client and one of the hardest working, most successful players in the history of professional golf. He and Christy have been married for many years and have three teenagers. Midway through dinner, Tom got up and left the room to take a phone call. One of the other guests turned to Christy.

"While Tom's away," he said, "let me ask you a question. If you told Tom he had to choose between you and golf, what would he say?"

Christy glared at the man a little.

"I'd never be so silly as to ask that question," she said.

"Why?" the provocateur persisted. "Are you afraid he might choose golf?"

"No," Christy replied. "But when I fell in love with Tom, part of the reason I loved him was because he was so passionately committed to golf. I can't imagine Tom without his love for golf. But Tom's never made it a competition between golf and me. He's always been able to love me and golf, to love our kids and golf, to love his parents and my parents and golf. I would never be so silly as to make him choose."

The wisdom of Christy's answer profoundly impressed me. It helped crystallize some thoughts and observations about the way people with real talent conduct their lives. *People with real talent usually manage to surround themselves with people who support their quest to make the most of their talent, whether it be in golf or any other endeavor. They show appreciation for that support. They cherish it.*

Of course, the first lessons I learned in this area came from my parents, especially my mother, Laura Rotella. Like my grandparents, my mother was an immigrant. Her family left England when she was a year old and settled on a farm in Michigan. Then they moved to Hornell, New York. When World War II broke out, she joined the Navy as a WAVE, serving as a dental hygienist. She and my father met at Bainbridge, Maryland, where he was teaching aircraft recognition to trainees. They fell in love, married, and were blessed with five kids.

My mother is the kind of person who will be a little embarrassed to see her name in the pages of this book. She tells me that she doesn't think she did anything special, that she just raised her family by doing the best she could and using the seat-of-the-pants wisdom she learned from her own family. She says she feels lucky that her children have turned out happy and successful.

My brothers, my sisters, and I saw it differently. We saw a woman who didn't count on luck. We saw a woman who was up every morning at six o'clock, cooking and cleaning and helping us get off to school. We saw a woman who was still working at 11:00 in the evening, when she went to bed.

We saw a woman who abhorred laziness in herself or in us. When we were very young, she worked only in our home, though when we were older she had jobs in a department store and with the University of Vermont's agricultural extension service. Whether she had an outside job or not, she worked. She sewed. She cooked delicious meals on a modest budget. She practiced economies that are all but lost arts today, like canning. She used to pay us ten cents a quart for wild blackberries we could find in our backyard. She'd put them up, along with vegetables from our backyard garden, until our shelves were full. We'd eat her blackberry pie, tarts, and jam all winter.

She wouldn't let her children be idle. If she saw one of us hanging around the house, she'd find a chore for us to do, which may be one reason I gravitated early to sports. She insisted that we do our chores well. My sister Mary Anne remembers that not only did she have to sweep floors but she also had to sweep them correctly.

She corrected our homework and insisted that we do our

best in school. Like our Dad, she believed that education would open up opportunities for us, and she was right. She wanted us to have choices in life because she understood that if we could choose careers that we loved, we had a better chance to be happy.

My brother Guy, who teaches at Northeastern University, told me recently that he still applies what my parents taught us about criticism when he works with his creative writing classes. My mother and father both had a knack for combining criticism with encouragement in a way that made a child believe he coud do better and want to get better. With my mother, it was always, "You did this well, but here's something you could do better."

She taught us moral lessons as well. God help the Rotella child whose behavior at school elicited a complaint from one of the teachers at a PTA meeting. There was no question whose side my mother would be on. She expected us to be honest, to speak politely, and to respect our elders. If we violated these tenets, we held out our hands for a rap from one of her wooden spoons, though as we grew older, we found we could make her laugh by smiling through one of these gentle punishments. That, however, risked the invocation of her ultimate sanction, which was to let Dad know what we had done.

By example, she showed us that material things were not the object of life. She had few expectations in the way of houses, cars, and clothing, and was pleased with what she received. She wanted very little for herself and she genuinely took pleasure in doing things for others.

She saw herself as part of a partnership with my father, and she made changes in her own life to support that partnership. She was a Methodist when she met my father, but she converted to Catholicism. And she did it wholeheartedly, becoming a devout Catholic. She adjusted to the numbers and culture of a big Italian family. She did whatever she could do to ease the burden and responsibilities my father carried. She even, in her sixties, took up golf because that was something he wanted to do.

She taught us, as my sisters sum it up, how to love. As I look back, I remember a feeling of being loved unconditionally. That didn't mean we were never punished, never disciplined. We were. But we never doubted that our parents loved us, that they would always be available when we needed help. We got a sense of security and a strong wish never to let down or disappoint the sources of that security.

I think of my mother as an enabler. That's a word that's been saddled with negative connotations by its association with alcohol and drug abuse. But an enabler doesn't have to be someone who supports a bad habit. An enabler can support the best in the people around him or her. That's the kind of enabler my mother is—an enabler of dreams for her husband and children.

I know, of course, that times have changed since my parents married. Women nowadays want and deserve an equal chance to pursue a career outside the home if that is where their dreams take them. Both of my sisters, Mary Anne and Susan, are successful businesswomen in ways that my mother never was.

But the fact remains that people who are successful, people who live lives of health, happiness, and achievement, tend to do it in partnership with someone who supports their dreams, who loves the passion and ambition in them.

In some cases, these partnerships follow the traditional paradigm in which the man occupies himself primarily with a career and the woman occupies herself primarily with home and family. But, thankfully, there are new paradigms today. We have couples in which the woman is the primary breadwinner and the man stays at home, tends to the family, and supports his spouse's dream. We have couples in which both spouses pursue challenging careers.

This means, above all, that couples must communicate and that they must make conscious, careful choices. A man can no longer assume that any woman he falls in love with will be willing to make the kinds of decisions my mother made. He has to make sure. Women and men who want to devote themselves primarily to a home and family are out there, but they don't wear labels. You have to talk to them and find out what they want.

If you, for example, intend to pursue a career that will re-

quire you to work long into the night on many occasions, it
behooves you to find a spouse who does not expect you home
for dinner every night at six o'clock. If you want a career that
requires lots of travel, don't marry someone who can't stand
to spend an evening alone.

And if you are fortunate enough to find and win a spouse
who enables you to chase your dream, who supports and loves
your passion for excellence, for heaven's sake appreciate it! I
am sometimes asked for counsel by professional golfers
whose games and marriages are both headed in the wrong direction. These are often men who have married women who
want to see them reach the top, who put their own career aspirations on hold to follow their husbands from tournament
to tournament. These men expect their wives to watch them
play during the day, then go back to the motel room at night
and listen to them moan and whine about their putting, and
the strength of the competition, and the likelihood that they
won't make enough money and will lose their Tour playing
privileges.

Then they're surprised when their wives start to question
their dreams.

I tell these guys that if they want their wives' support for
their dreams, they had better change their ways. Half an hour
or so is enough time for a discussion of what happened at
work every day, whether your work is golf or dry cleaning.
After that, it's up to you to make sure your spouse enjoys
the evening. You have to radiate optimism and happiness if

you expect your spouse to keep believing in your shared dream.

◆◯

The choices you make in a spouse and a career are especially important if children are part of your plan. Children require a lot of time from their parents. Nannies and day-care centers can be helpful, but they can't substitute for large increments of parental attention. If neither partner in a marriage is prepared to allot that time, that's fine. Let them each pursue all the career challenges they want. But they should consider carefully whether they really ought to and want to have children.

Let me make it clear that I don't advocate that one parent or another be the child-rearer and the other do nothing. That's not a paradigm that works. Both spouses, regardless of which one has the primary career, have to make sacrifices for the sake of the children. The touring golfers I work with all do this. A lot of them pass up lucrative Monday exhibition appearances so they can spend an extra day at home. They pass up tournaments they'd otherwise like to play in because they want to be home with their families, to play catch with the kids, and monitor their piano practice. They play in events they might otherwise pass up because the events coincide with school vacations and they know their wives and children can come along for the week.

Even so, there's no single, perfect solution I can offer to the problem of balancing career and family. All I know is there must be a balance. I certainly don't advocate neglecting family for the sake of a career. On the other hand, I've seen cases of people who neglect their jobs because they think they absolutely have to be at every Little League game.

That certainly wasn't true when I was growing up. I understood that my parents usually had more important, or at least more necessary, things to attend to than my football and basketball games. They came when they could, but I didn't feel neglected when they couldn't.

Nowadays, I find that my own daughter feels much the same. She plays tennis and golf for her high school teams. But she doesn't require or desire that I or my wife, Darlene, attend all of her matches. I think it's much more effective for me to help her practice and prepare than it is to watch her perform. Sometimes we lift weights together. Sometimes we work on specific golf or tennis shots. When I see her play golf, it's usually informal, when we're both practicing. Sometimes, I'll caddie for her when she plays a few holes at twilight. If she asks for advice, I'll offer some—but only if she asks.

Well, most of the time only when she asks.

It's wise to remember that your obligations to your children begin with love and support, discipline and moral values. But they include as well the economic essentials to get started in life—food, shelter, clothing, and education. Children also need role models, examples of how an adult with real talent lives his or her life.

159

There's a balance that will work in your family. You have to find it.

⚭

People with real talent, I've noticed, choose their friends in much the same way that they pick supportive spouses. If they work in an office, they go to lunch with colleagues who like their work, who are optimistic about their prospects, and who generally speak well of the company and the people who work there. They politely minimize contact with co-workers who tend to whine and complain.

This makes sense. Man is a social being. We have a strong tendency to want to get along with and agree with the people who share our lives. If you spend your lunch hour listening to a colleague talk about how hard the job is, how unfair the boss is, how unlikely success is, then you're very likely going to return to work feeling somewhat depressed, rather than energized for the rest of the day.

People with real talent also tend to appreciate their competitors rather than despise or denigrate them. Again, I learned a lot about this from Tom Kite. When I was beginning to work with tournament golfers, Tom was one of my first clients. Rather than try to keep what he learned from me to himself, Tom recommended me to other players on the Tour.

He explained to me that his objective was to see how good he could get. He saw the other players on the Tour as helpers in that quest, rather than enemies. They would push him to work harder on his game. The better they got, the better he would have to be. Tom figured there was enough prize money on the Tour to go around. He thought his life would be much more rewarding if he made friends with his competitors and even helped them get better. Over the years, I've seen that he was right.

People with real talent compete primarily against themselves. Their quest is to see how good they can get. They tend to get along well with their competitors.

I've also been fortunate in finding colleagues who taught me the right things about attitude and gave me invaluable support in my effort to become the best I could be at teaching golf's mental skills. Years ago, I was lucky enough to be invited to teach at *Golf Digest's* schools. The veteran professionals on the staff at those schools, men like Jim Flick and Davis Love, Jr., exuded the enthusiasm and commitment to teaching that I had seen in many great coaches. It turned out that this was an attitude established at the beginning in those schools by some of the best golfers ever to play the game, including Bob Toski and Paul Runyan. They were both well past their playing primes when I met them, but I have always enjoyed learning from older, more experienced men.

It would be hard to find two more seemingly disparate personalities than Toski and Runyan. Toski is tough, aggressive, occasionally profane with his students, and very witty. Runyan is self-effacing and soft-spoken, serious, given to explaining the game in terms of its geometry.

But they share some common traits and beliefs. They are passionately curious about how the game is played and taught. They are dogged in their determination to help the people they work with. They believe anyone can improve. During the years I taught at the *Golf Digest* schools, I played a lot of golf with them, shared a lot of meals with them. And while they taught me many things about the game, a lot of techniques and skills, what I remember most is what they taught me about attitude. It was impossible to work with them and not go out to the lesson tee feeling excited about the work ahead of us.

So it is, I think, in all endeavors. Everyone, no matter what his or her profession, can benefit from observing the principle behind what Harvey Penick used to say to pupils playing tournament golf:

"Don't go to dinner with bad putters."

CHAPTER ELEVEN

Hitting Your Prime After Fifty

Back in 1954, a salesman named Ray Kroc took a business trip from his home in Chicago to San Bernardino, California.

Kroc was at that time a moderately successful man. He sold machines that mixed milk shakes, and he'd done well enough with them to have a house in the suburbs and a few of the perks of the good life. But sales were flat. He could sense that the soda fountains and cafés that were the bulk of his market were a fading presence in the American economy. They were stuck in downtown areas while more and more Americans were moving to the suburbs.

Ray Kroc had visited thousands of little restaurants and seen many of them fail. He had a theory about why they failed that went beyond their location. One restaurant might have a good cook, but the owner might know nothing about purchasing. Another would go through a string of short-order cooks.

Its quality would rise and fall depending on the strengths and weaknesses of the individual cooks. No two restaurants seemed to make an egg salad sandwich exactly the same way. Beyond that, a given restaurant might make its egg salad one way one day and another way the next. Customers, who tend to like reliable quality, would drop away.

Then Kroc heard about a restaurant out in San Bernardino that was not only surviving, but thriving. It ordered and re-ordered Kroc's milk shake machines; in fact, it kept eight of them going at the same time. This was so unusual in the small-restaurant business at the time that Kroc decided to fly out to California to take a look.

What he found was a busy little hamburger stand owned by two brothers named McDonald. For a day or so, he sat in his car and observed. He saw a place that was clean, efficient, and inexpensive. He spoke to some of the customers, many of whom stayed in the parking lot and ate in their cars. He found that they thought eating at McDonald's beat tipping diner waitresses for serving inconsistent food. It beat bringing a cold meat loaf sandwich from home for lunch.

Kroc went inside and introduced himself to the McDonald brothers. What he saw impressed him further. The McDonalds had stripped their menu down to a few essentials—burgers, fries, shakes, soft drinks. They had devised a standardized, sensible way to prepare each of them. French fries, for instance, came from potatoes that were aged in a special bin that allowed air to circulate around them. They were peeled so as to leave a certain amount of skin around each piece. Then they were bathed in water, blanched, and fried. People loved them. And they got the same French fries every time.

It was the same way with hamburgers. Each patty weighed precisely the same as the next patty, had the same fat content, and was cooked the same way.

The systematization extended beyond the kitchen to the utensils, plates, and condiments, all the way to the schedule for cleaning the parking lot.

The McDonald brothers had hit upon a process that led to success, a process of the sort we've discussed earlier. Ray Kroc's brilliance lay in the fact that he recognized its potential.

The McDonald brothers, as it happened, weren't very interested in franchising the business themselves. They liked their small and prosperous niche in San Bernardino. But Ray Kroc could see the potential, and he left California with a deal that allowed him to set up and sell franchises that would use the McDonald name and methods. In his early years, he went to great lengths to ensure that every franchise did the essentials the same way. Eventually, the company set up its own school to teach those methods.

You know the rest.

I cite this story not to suggest that the food at McDonald's is the best around. I'm not even suggesting that many Americans didn't eat better and more nutritiously back in the days before the proliferation of fast food chains.

I cite this story because at the time he discovered McDonald's, Ray Kroc was fifty-two years old.

The stage was set for Ray Kroc to have a discontented middle age, to become the kind of guy whose income declined, who took an early and not very comfortable retirement, and who spent his time sitting in the men's grill at the club, playing pinochle for pennies with some cronies and muttering about how the world was going to hell—if he could afford to maintain his club membership.

But Kroc rewrote the scenario. He reinvented his business and the reinvented business reinvigorated him. He worked well into his eighties. When he died he left behind one of the world's largest companies and the San Diego Padres baseball team—all accumulated during the portion of his life when most people start to slow down.

That's a characteristic of people with real talent. They constantly find new ways to challenge themselves, new ways to invigorate themselves, especially when they reach middle age. They avoid burnout.

You don't have to be middle-aged to apply this principle. Ted Turner was in his mid-twenties when he discovered it.

He had had an inauspicious boyhood. His father, who owned a billboard company with signs in Tennessee and Georgia, was a heavy drinker and a troubled man. When Ted was home, his father applied discipline with everything from a wire hanger to a razor strop. But Ted wasn't home very often. From the age of ten or so, he spent most of his time in military boarding schools. He was thrown out of one of them for disciplinary problems. He wore out shoes at the other doing punishment marching for disciplinary demerits.

He didn't show a lot of promise in his extracurricular activities, either. His father provided him with sailboats to race, but he capsized so often his nickname was "Turnover Ted." The names Ted chose for his boats—*The Black Cat* and *Pariah*—give you some idea of what the boy thought of himself.

He was admitted to Brown University, but he was a disciplinary problem there as well. He was arrested twice. He got himself thrown out of his fraternity for burning its homecoming display. He left school well short of graduation.

He went to work for his father's billboard company. At about that time, the elder Turner floated a large loan for expansion into new states. But his father was deeply depressed, and within a year or two he made careful suicide plans. As part of the plan, he agreed to sell his new acquisitions to relieve the company of debt. That way, he figured, his wife and ex-wife would inherit an unencumbered estate. Then he shot himself.

In his early twenties, Ted Turner inherited control of a company that was about to get much smaller. It seemed as if, from the grave, his father was saying he wouldn't amount to anything. The decision to sell his new assets and retire his debt before he shot himself stated clearly that he didn't trust Ted to

167

run the company successfully enough to preserve the inheritance he wanted to leave to his family.

From that time on, Ted Turner had a mission. He successfully derailed the sale of assets his father had arranged. He worked like a demon to make the company succeed. By his late twenties, Turner had one of the larger and more successful billboard companies in the South.

People who knew him as a boy might have predicted that Ted Turner, once he had salvaged the billboard business, would start to coast and revert to the dissolute behavior patterns he'd shown in college. They would have been wrong.

Turner had discovered something about himself. He was capable of great achievement when he was motivated. He needed crises and disapproval and skeptics to motivate him.

"I just love it when people say I can't do something," he said. "There's nothing that makes me feel better, because all my life people have said I wasn't going to make it."

He embarked on a business expansion that in many ways replicated the situation his father had left him when he committed suicide. He borrowed heavily to acquire some radio stations and an obscure UHF television station, Channel 17 in Atlanta. He created a crisis for himself in which bankruptcy was a real threat.

Under that threat, Turner again worked like a demon. He generated money from the television and radio stations that the previous owners had not been able to earn. He saw the potential of cable and turned Channel 17 into a "superstation," WTBS, available all across the country.

Then he went out and repeated the pattern. When the television station began to work, he bought the moribund Atlanta Braves. When the Braves' fortunes improved, he bet everything again on Cable News Network. Then he leveraged that to buy MGM's film library. Finally, he merged the whole she-bang with Time Warner, a heavily indebted communications giant whose stock was disappointing analysts.

Now, in his late fifties, he's arranged to make himself vice chairman of Time Warner. Given Turner's history, I suspect two things. One is that he does not expect to be vice chairman indefinitely. And the other is that he does not expect the company's stock to be a sluggish performer very long.

◆◯

On the other hand, it's all too easy to lose in your middle age what you've built. Berry Gordy, the founder of Motown Records, lost control of his company less than thirty years after he started it.

In the early days, Gordy, as I've mentioned, had some setbacks along the way to fulfilling his dream of being a success in the music business. His record store failed. The songs he wrote impressed no one. He went to work in a factory fastening upholstery and chrome strips to Lincoln Continentals. But he was in close contact with the music of Detroit's black

169

community. One day he heard a singer named Smokey Robinson and he knew he was hearing something special.

He discovered a niche for himself. He began producing, recording, and editing the music being made by people like Smokey Robinson. He found that he could be a tenacious promoter. He could walk into the big radio stations in strange cities and persuade the disk jockeys that they ought to be playing Motown Records. And this was in the days when radio stations with white audiences played little if any music by black artists.

Soon he bought an old house for his company and put a sign on the front facade that read, "Hitsville, U.S.A." Talented people started knocking on the door. One of them was a group called Diane Ross and the Primettes. He suggested that they alter the lead singer's first name slightly and change their name to the Supremes. He discovered the Four Tops, the Temptations, Stevie Wonder, and the Jackson Five.

Gordy did more than that. He hired old vaudeville hoofers to teach Motown singers how to dance and present themselves on stage. He hired coaches to teach them diction and etiquette. He attracted brilliant songwriters to write music for them. He promoted them with tours and concert appearances. He was a constant presence in the entire creative process. Motown made him and many artists wealthy.

But it didn't last. One reason was competition. Once the established record companies saw the profits Motown was making, they started offering lucrative contracts to some of

Motown's best talent. They started scouting for and signing new black artists.

But that wasn't the main reason for Motown's decline. The main reason was Berry Gordy's declining interest. As the company grew, he found he had to pay more and more attention to contracts and finance and less and less to music and talent. He didn't like that. Then he fell in love with Diana Ross and spent a few years devoting most of his time to producing her movies. He moved the company's headquarters to Los Angeles, far from its roots.

In effect, he decided he could let the record business coast. It turned out that he couldn't. Eventually, the company went through a series of financial crises and he had to sell it.

As he did so, he was at least honest with himself. The real reason for the company's decline, he wrote, was not intensified competition or the financial and marketing advantages of large entertainment conglomerates. "The real reason was, I was just tired. I didn't want to do it anymore. It had long stopped being fun for me."

Those words could have been written by a myriad of middle-aged workers who falter in their work just as Berry Gordy faltered in his, only not so publicly. The business world and the academic world both have their share of experienced workers who aren't performing as well as they did when they were younger.

In an ironic sense, this validates the idea that real talent is more important in performance than the so-called talent

171

that's measured on tests. Measurable talent is barely affected by age. Your IQ is the same at sixty as it was when you were twenty. And you would think that, all other things being equal, people's performances would steadily improve throughout their careers as they accumulated more and more experience and gained more and more wisdom. The fact that performance sometimes declines in middle age testifies to the importance of motivation and enthusiasm, which are attributes of real talent.

It's not hard to understand why motivation can atrophy. To begin with, many professions have an apprenticeship period that is designed to identify and reward the best and the brightest young people. If you're a lawyer, you go through three years of school and then five or six years of work as an associate before you can be promoted to partner. If you teach at a university, you get your doctorate and then you teach for a few years as an assistant professor before you can be considered for tenure.

Naturally, people work hard during this apprenticeship. They understand that a cut is going to be made at about the age of thirty. If they want the security and perks of tenure or partnership or whatever it's called in their profession, they have to work hard. Some may be motivated by the intense desire not to fail in clearing this important hurdle.

Even after the first hurdle is past them, people in their thirties still see important goals. They want promotions or recognition within their fields. The ladder still looks climbable.

The view from the top looks inviting. At the same time, people in their twenties and thirties usually have major material incentives. They want to buy homes and cars and to provide for their children.

But by the age of fifty or so, the perception changes. Because of the pyramidal nature of most companies, there isn't likely to be a lot of upward mobility for a manager in his fifties. A company has room for lots of junior executives in their twenties. It has room for only a handful in their fifties.

And the major material needs are mostly behind you. The house has been bought, if not completely paid for. The cars are in the garage. The kids are through with college, or close to it. The check for the initiation fee at the club was written years ago.

Moreover, the learning curve for many people has flattened out by the time they reach their fifties. If you're a White House reporter, for example, you are constantly learning during the first administration you cover and you're excited by the novelty. By the time your fourth president comes around, you've seen it all. You no longer get excited when you're called into the briefing room. If you're a lawyer, the fifteenth merger you handle starts to look a lot like the fourteenth.

These are the conditions that prompt some people to burn out.

It used to be that companies and institutions routinely carried nonproductive older employees. A few still do, but their number is diminishing. In today's ruthlessly competitive economy, less productive older employees are the first ones managers look for when they get orders to downsize. Even situations that once looked secure, like partnership in a law firm, no longer are safe havens. If you're a partner in a law firm and you're not bringing in business and generating income, you've got barely more job security than the average associate.

Some of the companies I consult with have a policy that takes into account an older employee's attitude. If you've been a loyal, productive worker for thirty years and you've started to slump, you probably won't be terminated if your attitude remains good—that is, if you are a good influence in the office, the kind of person who's enthusiastic about what the younger people are doing, who's enthusiastic about the company itself, who offers sound advice and sets a good example. It's not unlike what the University of Virginia athletic program does with seniors who aren't going to play much, if at all. If the senior nevertheless sets a good example at practice, always hustles, and is a positive influence on the team, he or she keeps the scholarship.

But if you're the type of older employee who gripes and whines and starts to infect younger employees with your bad attitude, no company is going to carry you these days. And why should it? The company's first responsibility is to itself and its stockholders. Companies which carry too many non-productive employees can't stay in business.

People with real talent, though, never run much risk of being offered early retirement because they look for and find new challenges in their fifties. Maybe, like Ray Kroc, they start an entirely new business of their own. Maybe, like Ted Turner, they expand an existing business in a way that gives them the feeling that they're starting all over again. There are a lot of arguments to be made for this approach. It's one way to capitalize on the experience and wisdom you've accumulated in thirty-odd years in the marketplace. If you're not already a CEO, it's one way to see how you can perform in that role. But there are obvious risks involved and I wouldn't make a blanket recommendation that everyone who's fifty and feeling a little burned out become a venture capitalist.

The key thing is to find ways to challenge yourself. Some people do that by switching, say, from a sales job to a management and training position. They find they enjoy passing along what they've learned. Others might switch their focus from individual clients to big, corporate accounts. Others might switch careers entirely. Any of these is better than stagnating.

It might simply be that you know that people generally start to slow down at the age of fifty-five because they lose their desire. So you decide to separate yourself from the crowd by getting even more enthusiastic and more committed as you get older.

Or it could be that you understand that aging is itself a challenge. It's not one that you can ultimately defeat, of course. But you can fight a long holding action against age. That holding action begins with the realization that if you want to feel

175

young, you have to think like a younger person. You must have the zeal and enthusiasm you had in your youth.

Even if you want to switch your priorities away from work as you move toward retirement, you can find a challenge. Suppose you'd like to improve your golf game. You want to get out of the office every day at three o'clock to practice and play. That becomes your incentive for being extremely effective and efficient during the six or seven hours you are in the office. That's fine with me. People ought to know how to be more productive in less time in their fifties, because they've got experience to help them.

I have a client from Cincinnati who makes an extremely good living as a financial consultant. He used to work as an engineer for Procter & Gamble. He understands the company and its compensation package. He knows that there are thousands of P&G employees interested in advice on how to invest the profit-sharing revenues they receive. He provides that advice.

A few years ago he decided to take a half day off a week. He found that business nevertheless went up. The next year he started taking a full day off. Business still went up. He started taking a day and a half off per week and giving his staff a half day off. Business went up yet again. Admittedly, the middle years of this decade have not been the hardest period in history for doing well in the financial services business. But the phenomenon of getting more accomplished in less time is something most older workers could experience.

Remember that it's not about having experience. It's about how you respond to your experience. Ask yourself some questions. Are you getting better or getting bitter? Are you juiced or are you stale? Are you hungrier or are you coasting?

And remember this: *You can only coast in one direction.*

CHAPTER TWELVE

Recruiting Real Talent

One of the smartest decisions the University of Virginia athletic department ever made was the hiring of Bruce Arena to coach soccer. It happened almost by accident.

Bruce was an All-America in lacrosse while he was at Cornell. He was All–Ivy League in soccer. After college, he played several years of professional lacrosse and soccer before the university hired him. Lacrosse, then and now, was a premier sport at Virginia. The team contended every year for the national championship. Bruce was told, when he came aboard in 1978, that his primary job was going to be assistant lacrosse coach.

Almost as an afterthought, he was given the job of coaching soccer. Soccer then was a minor sport at Virginia. There was little or no recruiting. The team generally broke about even. "They wanted me to baby-sit the soccer program," Bruce recalls. "They wanted a nice, healthy program where the kids had a good time."

That, of course, was one of the reasons the team was not particularly outstanding. The kids were too intent on having a good time.

Bruce was not about to baby-sit a mediocre program. He tells me that his parents instilled in him the idea that there was a correct way and a wrong way to do anything, and anything he put his name to had to be done correctly—whether it involved making his bed or cutting the lawn or coaching a soccer team. He thought that Virginia's tolerance of mediocrity in soccer and other sports was inexcusable. He was determined to change it.

But Bruce's options with the soccer program were limited. The traditional path of upward mobility in American college soccer went overseas. Coaches recruited accomplished foreign players. Bruce didn't like that option. For one thing, he didn't have much of a recruiting budget, certainly not enough for scouting trips abroad. For another, Charlottesville in the 1970s was a bit more insular and provincial than it is today. He didn't think he could honestly tell a foreign athlete he would fit in well.

Bruce decided to focus his recruiting on areas within a day's drive or so of Charlottesville. Given where soccer was played seriously in those days, that meant he was going to be looking mostly at kids from the Washington, Baltimore, Philadelphia, and New York areas.

And he wouldn't be able to pick and choose among the best players in that region, either. He was a new coach from a school with no soccer history and a mediocre record in the sport. He had few scholarships to hand out. He wasn't going to be running into any high school All-Americas who had always dreamed of playing soccer for Virginia. He wasn't going to be able to lure many players with free rides. He was going to have to start with players who might have been overlooked by the collegiate soccer powerhouses. He was going to have to persuade them to come to Virginia with little or no scholarship aid.

But what he could do, given the limited geographic area he was working in, and given his passionate desire to succeed, was scout the kids he recruited very carefully. And that gave him an opportunity to evaluate whether a potential recruit had real talent.

Bruce recognized that in a program like his, real talent was critical. The kids with obvious physical talent were going to be playing for other schools. He had to come up with kids who compensated for their lesser physical talents with their attitude, their desire, their discipline, their will to win, their ability to fit into a team, and their commitment to improvement.

Many college coaches and some managers in the business world are aware of the importance of real talent. But they don't always recruit people with real talent. The main reason, as we've discussed, is that real talent is hard to measure. Conventional talent is easy to measure. The kid who leads the state in goal scoring for his high school soccer team isn't always the one with the most real talent. But if you're a coach with limited recruiting resources, you'll be strongly tempted to recruit that kid anyway. If he doesn't work out, you can always say, "Hey, he led the state in scoring his senior year. Who could tell he wouldn't make it at the college level?" That excuse is a little easier to sell than "He wasn't the biggest star in high school, but I thought he had a great attitude." In the same way, a business recruiter who wants to cover his backside rather than run risks to recruit real talent can always justify hiring the kid with the best GPA in his business school class.

Bruce didn't care about his backside. He wanted to win soccer games. He was committed to doing whatever he could to make that happen. Given his resources, the recruiting process had to be thorough. That meant spending long hours on the road, watching kids play soccer, talking to kids, evaluating their games and their attitudes.

One of the things he did was discount the record a boy made on his high school soccer team. Bruce was more interested in what kids did for their club soccer teams. There were several reasons for this. One was that the clubs generally played a better brand of soccer than the high school teams. So if a player accomplished something on the club level, Bruce knew it meant something. He appreciated the skills and experience a boy brought out of a top-flight club program. A kid might do great things in high school soccer that were more a reflection of the caliber of the competition than of his own ability.

But there were attitudinal factors as well at work in Bruce's decision to focus on club players. Playing on a club team be-spoke a level of commitment and discipline. It meant that a boy was dedicated to working on soccer year-round, or nearly year-round. It meant that he had to make time for practice in odd places at odd hours. It meant that he accepted and thrived on the kind of regimen the coach of a top-flight club de-manded.

He understood something that I think is very important in scouting for real talent. You have to look for signs in a poten-tial recruit's background, such as joining a soccer club, that the individual is self-motivated.

Sometimes people achieve things because they're pushed and prodded all the way. Some high school and college football and basketball players are like this. Coaches keep them on a very tight leash. They yell at them on the practice field. They yell at them in the weight room. They assign someone to walk them to class and someone to work with them in a mandatory study hall at night. Crowds cheer for them on game day. As a result, the individual may perform impressively, both acade-mically and athletically. But his performance may not be rooted in real talent. Some nonathletes have analogous back-grounds. They get good grades because they respond to the prodding of their parents and teachers. That doesn't mean they have real talent.

If your job involves recruiting and you're looking for people with real talent, you'd probably be better off looking for an athlete who had to join a club or take some initiative to play, perhaps for an athlete who made his mark in a minor sport like wrestling or cross-country. This is far more likely to be someone whose accomplishments come from his or her own inner resources. Or you might, as Bob Sherman at Merrill Lynch does, look for students who have displayed leadership in extracurricular activities. Again, this is something that stems from an individual's own initiative.

Bruce Arena devised ways to separate players with real talent from those who didn't have it. He watched kids until, eventually, he saw them play on a bad day, a day when they weren't shooting well or were up against a top-notch defender. He looked for the kids who found ways to pick up their games on their bad days by playing better defense, scrambling for loose balls, sacrificing themselves to set someone else up for a chance to score, finding ways to help their teams.

He tried to watch his prospects until he saw them in a game where their team lost badly. He wanted to see how a player reacted to adversity. Some kids told the story with their body language. Their shoulders slumped. They stopped being aggressive. Others displayed tenacity even in a hopeless cause.

Bruce found ways to assess character in the conversations he had with potential recruits. Any kid who was smart enough to qualify academically for admission to Virginia had by that time already learned to say what coaches like to hear. So Bruce discounted it when a kid said that he wanted to work hard and hustle all the time and just have a chance to play.

But after he'd seen a boy play a few games and had formed a

good impression of his strengths and weaknesses as a player, Bruce would ask the player to assess his own game. He compared the boy's answer to his own impressions. If the boy perceived and admitted the weaknesses Bruce had perceived, Bruce concluded that the boy had one of the essential ingredients of a good attitude: he was honest in his self-evaluation. Bruce finds it's possible to work with and improve a player who acknowledges his flaws. It's almost impossible to improve one who doesn't.

He made it a point to get to know a potential recruit's parents. And he listened to what the parents said. If they talked only of how much scholarship money he might be able to give their boy, he got wary. He wanted to hear parents ask about the education their son would be getting. He wanted to know that a boy he recruited had imbibed strong and sensible attitudes at home.

Occasionally, of course, Bruce saw a player who was so skilled that he took him despite being less than impressed with his attitude. But he imposed strict limits on that. He took no more than one person per year with a suspect attitude. More than that, he thought, could spoil the atmosphere around the team.

And the atmosphere was a very important part of Bruce's coaching philosophy. He knew that a team performs best when its leadership is internal, when it comes not just from the coaches, but from the players themselves.

It begins, he believes, with his own performance. "You are the kids' first role model," he says. "You have to demonstrate the attitudes you want in the way you conduct yourself—your honesty, your commitment, your discipline."

But once he had recruited a preponderance of players with real talent, Bruce found that a lot of his concerns took care of themselves. The seniors and juniors on the team let the newcomers know, by example, what was expected of them. The soccer team changed from one that began practice when school started in September and disbanded after the last game in November to a year-round operation. The players worked indoors during the winter. They scrimmaged in the spring. They joined summer clubs. They lifted weights. They had a work ethic. The team began to win.

At that point, Bruce reaffirmed something all good coaches know. "Success is contagious," as he puts it. "There's no room for a kid to slack off. You have a system, a work ethic. You're expected to do your job."

He was able to raise the level of his recruiting. He still looked for boys with real talent—discipline, commitment, honesty about their games. But he was now able to recruit players with great physical gifts as well, players who have gone on from Virginia to star in major league soccer, for the United States national team, and for European professional clubs.

He continued to recruit kids who weren't considered top-flight talent. He gave them the opportunity to walk on to his teams without scholarships. And because they had great attitudes, a number of them did. They made major contributions to Bruce's teams.

Bruce began to win on an unprecedented scale in college soccer. He won five NCAA championships. In 1996, he coached the United States Olympic team. Then he became coach of D.C. United, the Washington franchise in the new American professional soccer league. His team won the league title its first two years. He's just become coach of the United States team for the next World Cup.

Bruce tells me that he still employs the same principles in recruiting and scouting on the professional level. He's still looking for players with real talent—players with character. He has a few players with great physical skills on his team. Among the rest, attitude is a critical factor.

"If you have one player with attitude problems, it's bad," Bruce says. "If you have two it's much worse." Some general managers and coaches ruin their teams by taking on too many players with million-dollar bodies and ten-cent heads. Bruce doesn't risk that. He finds and recruits character.

I have seen this emphasis on recruitng character time and again in the sport and business world. I talked recently with Danny Wilmer, the football recruiting coordinator at Virginia. Danny has been in Charlottesville sixteen years, years during which the program has risen from mediocrity to consistent excellence. Before that, he recruited at James Madison University, where he discovered future NFL stars like Charles Haley and Gary Clark.

Danny says the Virginia football coaches have some minimal size and speed requirements for each position on a football team, just as there are minimal grades and test scores. Lots of potential recruits meet those physical and academic standards.

But in winnowing that large group down to the two dozen or so who are offered football scholarships every year, the coaching staff relies heavily on its assessment of character traits that are part of real talent. Danny refers to a potential player's work ethic. Does he lift weights, work during the off-season, do the things that will make him a stronger, faster athlete? Is he a leader?

These are not easy things to evaluate, and they've become more difficult because of recruiting restrictions imposed by the NCAA. Where Bruce Arena could go see a prospect many times and watch his reactions to many different circumstances, football coaches now may watch a recruit play only once. Their visits and talks are limited as well. The coaches can view film, but cameras can't see into a boy's heart.

That's why it's important for the football program to have an experienced recruiting coordinator like Danny Wilmer. Over the years, Danny has built an extensive network of friends and contacts who know high school athletics throughout Virginia and the other states in which the University recruits. Some are coaches. Some are principals and assistant principals. There are even a few janitors, Danny says. Over the years, he's learned which ones can be counted on for a reliable assessment of a boy's character.

When he is rating a prospect, Danny consults this network. Sometimes he'll hear that a boy has a great work ethic and a fine character. That boy goes to the top of the list. Sometimes he'll hear that a boy is essentially all right and should benefit from a change of scenery and new friends in Charlottesville. That boy doesn't get rated very highly for leadership. He goes into a middle category. And sometimes he hears that a kid has terrible work habits and gets by on physical ability alone. I'm not going to suggest that such a player is automatically dropped from the list. Coaches from Knute Rockne on down have found that they can afford to carry one or two players with questionable attitudes if their physical talents are truly extraordinary. But if the physical talent is just a hair less than extraordinary or there are already too many bad attitudes on the team, a coach is well advised to drop such a player into the "do not recruit" category.

But in football, soccer, or any endeavor, successful managers find that half their battle is won if they can identify and recruit people with real talent.

The recruiting process is a little different in the business world. There's no NCAA counting the number of contacts a manager has with a prospect. So the best managers I know of take the time to evaluate job applicants for real talent.

I've spoken already of Phil Blevins, the manager of Merrill Lynch's highly successful office in Washington, D.C. Phil has recruited hundreds of financial consultants as he's built his office's business. He considers recruiting and evaluating talent to be just as important as managing the brokers already on board at Merrill Lynch. He doesn't delegate the job to a personnel office or a screening device. "It's one of the most important things I do," he explains. "Why should I leave it to a personnel officer with two years' experience?"

Like Danny Wilmer, Phil finds that attitude is what separates good prospects from bad ones. There are many applicants with the requisite education, appearance, and IQ for the job. He's looking for the ones with the right attitudes. And while there are batteries of tests available to give applicants, Phil has found that personal contacts work best in assessing a prospect's attitudes. By the time they reach Merrill Lynch, applicants have been taking standardized tests for nearly twenty years. The smart ones can often figure out what a psychological test is looking for and fill in the requisite boxes with their No. 2 pencils. Some of them can finesse a first interview as well. That's why Phil has them back four or five times before he makes a hiring decision.

What does he look for?

"I don't hire off the résumé. Everyone looks great on a résumé," Phil says. "I look for coachability. That means they want to improve themselves and they're willing to listen and learn how to do it. I look for people who are hungry to be better than they are, to be something special in life. I look for people who aren't satisfied with being average. I look for people with energy and enthusiasm, people who are looking for excitement in their lives. I've never hired anyone for what they are. I hire them for what they can be. We're going up the mountain. Are they interested in getting to the top and willing to pay the price?"

This is not a science. Phil says there are a few things that will turn him off during this process, like a prospect who wants to know too much too soon about the employee benefit package. But it's hard to say what tells him that a prospect has what he's looking for. "It's a gut reaction," Phil will say. Sometimes the evaluation of real talent has to be that way.

Bruce Arena, Danny Wilmer, and Phil Blevins all recognize the critical importance of real talent in recruiting. They're all willing to put in the time to evaluate it. They don't take the easy way out of relying on test scores or easily measured physical abilities. That's one big reason why they and their organizations have all been so successful.

CHAPTER THIRTEEN

Unleashing Real Talent

A little while ago I learned that an old client of mine named Bob Collins was about to retire after thirty-eight years with General Electric. The news brought back some warm memories, because Bob gave me an opportunity to learn a lot about managing and nurturing real talent.

Bob first got in touch with me more than a dozen years ago, shortly after he came to Charlottesville to work as the chief of the industrial computers unit at a new entity within GE called the Factory Automation Division. His unit was losing money and he was having problems with morale. He'd heard about some of the work I'd been doing with the football and basketball teams at the University and he thought I might be able to help. He came over to my house. We talked for the better part of a day.

Bob had an impressive engineering background. He'd gone to work for GE straight out of Manhattan College's electrical engineering program. He'd spent most of his time in GE's aerospace projects. He couldn't tell me about this at the time, but his last major project in that area concerned the Stealth fighter development program. Bob's team had been charged with developing aircraft instrumentation for the Stealth, including such things as cockpit gauges and fuel monitors. They all had to be redesigned to fit into the Stealth's revolutionary radar-evading profile. They all had to withstand powerful pulses of electromagnetic energy, because the plane was intended for possible use in a nuclear conflict. It was a complex, rewarding task. Bob remembers that they knew they were getting things right when they sent the prototype planes up over Edwards Air Force Base in California at night. The air defense monitors at Edwards had no idea what was up there.

But Bob was smart enough to see that defense spending couldn't continue at the rates of the early 1980s. He had a sense that the Soviet Union would not be able to keep the pace and would fade as a threat to the United States. So he started looking for a transfer into civilian production, and that was what brought him to Charlottesville.

The Factory Automation Division represented an attempt by GE to claim a share of a small market, but a market the company thought would grow quickly. I won't go into the technical details, but the idea was to marry the computer to industrial machinery. If you have, for example, a toothpaste factory, you have machines that squirt toothpaste into tubes, put caps on them, and put the labels on the tubes. Until the 1980s, workers had to operate the machines. GE and others saw that a computer could be made to perform that task, turning the toothpaste machine on and off, regulating its speed, and so on. The workers would be free to be transferred to more productive assignments.

But the venture, which was by then about three years old, was not doing well. There was more competition for the division than GE had planned on. In addition to that, Bob told me, there were serious management problems that were affecting his unit's morale. He blamed himself for part of the problem.

For one thing, there were three units operating, supposedly independently, under one roof in Charlottesville. One was Bob's industrial computers group, with about sixty employees and sales of $7 million. Another was a laboratory. And the third was a robotics unit.

While Bob's unit had its problems, the other two had even more. They were frequently late meeting deadlines. They were losing far more money than GE found tolerable, even given allowances for a start-up venture.

But when the orders came for the division to cut costs, the orders were applied to all three units. That meant Bob's unit had to suffer layoffs. It had to postpone or forgo investments in new computers and equipment that the engineers felt they needed. Promised salary increases were deferred or canceled. Management, Bob thought, was excessively shortsighted, looking too closely at quarterly results and not paying enough attention to the longer term. "It's start-stop management," Bob told me. "There are lots of mixed signals, a lot of complaining and backbiting. There's a lack of cooperation."

As a result, morale in Bob's unit was not good. One of the problems, he realized, was that the atmosphere discouraged people from making complaints and suggestions. With some justification, they thought that people who stuck their necks out tended to get their heads chopped off. And, when praise and rewards were handed out, they tended to go to the managers of the various groups within the unit, rather than to the group members themselves. Many of the employees were consequently sullen and difficult to motivate.

Bob, in fact, found that only about 20 percent of his staff could be characterized as "go-to guys." For those not familiar with sports terminology, a go-to guy is someone you can rely on to perform well in a difficult situation, someone who's positive and enthused and productive. (He's the guy a basketball team "goes to," or gives the ball to, when they need someone to take the final shot in a close game.) The rest were below average in effectiveness.

Bob saw this as a tremendous, perhaps fatal, waste of resources. He realized that his venture could not succeed without harnessing the real talent of its employees. He knew that talent was there. He looked at the personnel files and saw that his staff had been successful in school. They'd been leaders of their teams and clubs. But in the environment at the Factory

Automation Division a lot of them had gotten discouraged. They'd lost their drive and their enthusiasm.

Bob had been trying for a year or more to turn things around when he came to see me. He was trying to break down some of the hierarchy and some of the mistrust in the unit, trying to change its style of management. For example, he wasn't calling his managers managers anymore. He was calling them coaches, because he wanted them to encourage and guide more than they criticized.

He acknowledged that he hadn't been entirely successful. He said he'd been too quick to criticize on occasion, too quick to blame. He'd removed a few people whom he probably should have helped and encouraged a little longer. "I've been a smoking-gun kind of manager," he said.

We talked that day about some of the things Bob would have to do personally if he wanted to turn the situation around. He would have to stop cutting people with his words and his facial expressions. He would have to convince them that he valued their suggestions and even their complaints. He'd have to assuage their fear of his quick trigger.

Bob impressed me with his candor, just as Virginia soccer recruits impressed Bruce Arena if they were capable of honest self-evaluation. And he persuaded me that there was indeed a tragic waste going on at the Factory Automation Division. Here was a talented and highly educated group of people positioned to take advantage of a lucrative new market. But they weren't doing it. Like Bob, I was impressed with the potential for growth in the company. I was convinced that they could reach that potential if they could bring their real talents to bear on their problems.

The first priority, we thought, had to be establishing trust within the unit. I was convinced that Bob and GE ultimately had the staff's best interests at heart. They all would benefit from a company that was productive and profitable. But the staff didn't feel that way.

So Bob arranged for me to meet with groups of his staff members without his presence. I told them what I believed— that Bob wanted to make changes that would benefit everyone and he wanted their input. "He wants to help you make great products and sell them all over the world," I said.

The people I spoke to were skeptical.

"How can we trust you?" one of them asked. "Are you here for Bob Rotella, Bob Collins, Jack Welsh [then chairman of GE], or what?"

"We're all in this together, the way I see it," I replied. "If I don't help you guys and Bob Collins, then I don't have any future here. And if Bob and I can't help you help us, then Jack Welsh is in trouble. You have one decision to make. You had some past leaders who didn't live up to your trust in them. But you can believe that Bob Collins told me that he wants me to find out what the problems are and have you help solve them. If you give up hope and refuse to trust him because you've been burned in the past, then we don't have a prayer. You'll teach Bob to be like all the other managers you've had."

They started to open up. Their complaints were what Bob suspected they would be. The inconsistency and mistakes of past management had destroyed much of their trust and loyalty. They didn't see any reason to believe Bob's promise that things would get better.

I said, "Well, I'm going to take your complaints to Bob and present them to him. We'll see what he says." And I did.

"Fantastic," Bob said when he heard the list of complaints I'd compiled. "That sounds like real stuff." That's not what you might expect to hear a manager say about complaints from his own staff. But Bob was anxious to establish better communication.

The next day, I met with the same engineers. I told them that Bob had read their complaints and did not disagree with them. The absence of any negative reaction on his part was telling. I told them that Bob wanted us to draw up a list of ten improvements the company could make.

That engendered more skepticism. But eventually, the group came up with a list. To their credit, it had little to do with their own personal needs. It had a lot to do with making them more efficient. Designers and software writers, for instance, wanted to streamline the process for acquiring new computers to help them work more efficiently. They said they wanted to know more about the company's long-term strategy. If they were going to work hard, they wanted to know where their work was taking them.

Bob called a meeting of the entire staff at a hotel away from the plant. He accepted the entire list. Some changes, he said, would be implemented immediately. Some would take longer. But they were all worth doing. He got a standing ovation.

As the meeting ended, I could see new enthusiasm on the faces of the staff. I continued to work for several more months as a facilitator of communication. But fairly soon, I wasn't needed. Bob and his people were talking to one another in a new way.

That period marked the beginning of a major change in the way Bob's unit was managed, a change that had a major impact on the attitudes of everyone in the operation. Some of the changes were symbolic. The unit established an across-the-board casual dress code. Coaches, as they were now called, no longer wore suits unless they had to to make a visiting customer comfortable. On the floor, they dressed just like everyone else.

The casual dress reinforced the point Bob was trying to make, which was that there was no longer going to be such a sharp distinction between salaried employees—the old managers—and hourly employees, the workers. They were all going to be part of the same team.

He found the dress change remarkably effective. Where once he had been treated deferentially and coolly on the floor when he wore a suit, he was now treated as a colleague. People talked to him about their problems and their ideas for solutions. He began to get much more input from the staff.

Some changes took longer to make than the new dress code. Bob needed a couple of years to respond fully to the staff's request for a better idea of where the company was headed. The response required that they take a searching look at the market they were trying to serve. It involved projections of investment and revenue. It was a much more market-oriented business plan than GE had originally had for the division. Once it was finally printed and distributed, Bob found that it gave a strong boost to creativity and motivation.

That is because people, as I've mentioned, tend to be much more confident and much more optimistic when they feel they can control, at least partially, their own situations, their own destiny. Having a long-range mission statement for the company that was drafted by people in the company helped give them that feeling.

At the same time, Bob reorganized the hierarchical structure of his unit. He broke it into task-oriented teams. He continued to redefine the job of his managers, still using the coaching analogy. In a nutshell, he asked them to switch from being cops to being advisers, facilitators, and guides. The goal was to make a majority of the employees go-to guys.

That kind of managerial attitude requires trust. Bob was prepared to give it. Where he had managers who couldn't adjust to the new style, he found them other jobs to do.

It required still more trust to respond to the staff's desire for more streamlined investment authorization, especially in a company with a recent history of drastic efforts to cut costs.

But Bob, again, was prepared to give it. He cut back on the number of signatures needed to purchase things like new computer workstations. This gave the staff more autonomy and still more sense that they controlled their own situations.

Bob reinforced that feeling by persuading GE to change the nature of the rewards system at the division. The new profit-sharing program for its employees reflected the way their unit had done, independently of other units or of GE as a whole. When he recognized superior achievement, he recognized teams more than individuals. He gave his coaches and even staff the authority to bestow instant rewards, like a company-paid dinner out, on individuals who deserved them.

Recognizing both the value of real talent and of his team concept, Bob revamped the hiring practices. Instead of having a personnel specialist and a supervisor interview a candidate, he started having group interviews in which many different staff members participated. Bob found that this helped identify candidates with real talent, candidates who would fit into the enthusiastic, team-oriented culture he was striving to build.

He built on the meeting we held at the local hotel, starting a regular schedule of "town meetings" for the staff. At one of the first of these, he took a major risk for himself by promising the staff that the era of layoffs was over. He kept that promise.

He set a great example with his own practices. Since much of the company's market was in Asia, Bob realized he was going to have to travel back and forth frequently to cultivate customers. He knew that frequent travel to the Far East could be wearing on a middle-aged body. So he altered his diet, emphasizing vegetables. He hired a trainer to help him improve his fitness. He disciplined himself to enable him to do the traveling the company required to succeed. His staff saw this dedication and responded to it.

Bob's example was characteristic of the successful managers I've seen. No one outworks them. Their dedication and commitment are contagious.

Bob would be the first to acknowledge that the generally buoyant economy of the past dozen years was also a factor in his company's growth. But a lot of companies have failed in the same time period. Few have grown as spectacularly as GE's Factory Automation Division.

By 1987, the division's staff had grown to more than 1,200 employees and sales were around $100 million. GE saw the critical importance of the Far East market for industrial machines. So it formed a joint venture with Fanuc, Ltd. of Japan and folded Bob's division into it. The joint venture was called GE Fanuc Automation, and Bob became the president and chief executive officer. Its staff now numbers 1,800 and its last annual sales figure was $600 million. That's a 600 percent increase in revenues over the past decade with only a 50 percent increase in staff.

It is, Bob says, a result of unleashing the hidden productivity, the real talent, in the staff.

I don't pretend to be an industrial management expert, but

it doesn't take an expert to see that there are lessons to be learned from Bob's experience for virtually any manager. One is that the day of hiring a labor force and treating them like automatons is over. Companies could get away with that, perhaps, in the days when a worker's job was largely manual, consisting, say, of repeatedly lugging a car door to an assembly line and fastening it to a frame. But the companies that will lead our economy into the next century have turned such chores over to machines, or soon will.

These enterprises will rely increasingly on highly educated, creative workers. Whether they write software or market securities or design automobiles, the quality of their work depends on their attitudes toward their work, on their self-discipline, their initiative, their commitment, and their enthusiasm. In short, it depends on whether they have real talent and whether the company nurtures that talent.

Every successful manager I speak with these days reinforces that message. I have worked for many years with Pat Walsh, a senior vice president at Merrill Lynch. He works in the human resources area.

As far as Pat is concerned, the single most important challenge facing Merrill Lynch is hanging on to its most productive financial consultants, the people with real talent. There is nothing that can devastate an office's performance faster than seeing three or four of its best men and women lured away by other companies. These are not the old days of industrial management when you simply put an ad in the paper to produce a pool of applicants able and eager to fill the slot of someone who quit. There is no way quickly or easily to replace your best producers. And other companies, looking for a quick way to improve their numbers, are constantly making offers to Merrill Lynch's stars.

This means that Merrill Lynch's managers have to create an atmosphere which makes the best people happy and encourages them to stay. It means that the days of the boss-as-martinet are over.

Good managers at Merrill Lynch create an atmosphere that inspires loyalty, in part, with the standard tools that any manager would use. They establish a comfortable, attractive, and efficient physical environment at the office. They provide the best support services they can. They look for opportunities to bestow rewards and recognition on top performers. They're eager and happy to help their people earn promotions. And they do the usual sorts of entertaining—taking people to lunch occasionally, holding a Christmas party.

But that's not enough.

Pat has searched for the right word to describe what managers have to provide in addition to those basics. He hasn't come up with the right one yet. The closest he can get is "affection."

A successful manager at Merrill Lynch these days, Pat feels, has to be a man or woman who truly is fond of the people he works with, who cares about them and their happiness, not just what they can add to the bottom line. It's not something that can be faked. People see through insincere efforts to pro-ject affection. Affection has to be demonstrated in dozens of small ways every day, from the first time a manager greets em-ployees in the hallway each morning to the pizza he buys for people staying late.

It's not something that can easily be taught. Pat tells me that Merrill Lynch has no manual or training program that teaches people how to do it. The company can only try to spot young executives with the requisite capacity for affection.

Of course, if all a manager had to have was affection, the company could simply go out and hire a bunch of sweet, car-ing grandmothers to run its offices. It's not that simple. Mer-rill Lynch is in a tough, competitive business and its managers have to convey and enforce the company's expectations. Sometimes, they have to let people go. No company these days can afford to carry a significant number of unproductive employees. Nor should it.

Pat, however, insists that Merrill Lynch never lose sight of the dignity of the person being let go. Such people are afforded opportunities to get counseling and help in finding new work. They get a financial bridge to help them. Occasionally, if this process works, they even express gratitude because deep in-side they know that the job wasn't suited to them and they're happy to be helped to find a job that is.

This, I think, makes a lot more sense than the sorts of crass, dehumanized downsizings that used to occur regularly in cor-porate America. I don't think it's any coincidence that some of the companies most famous for mass layoffs don't seem to be thriving these days. Mass layoffs don't exactly build loyalty among the people with real talent who are left.

Some of the things that worked for Bob Collins at GE Fanuc and for Pat Walsh at Merrill Lynch will work for almost any manager. People need to feel in control of as many things as possible if they are to be as confident and optimistic as they can be. They will produce best in such an atmosphere. It helps if they can see a direct link between the success of their work and their compensation. It helps if they can see a direct link between their efforts and the mission of the company. It helps if their leader sets a great example. It helps if they can sense affection and loyalty in the people who supervise them.

The employees of the next century need to recognize that the creative autonomy they will be granted by managers trying to nurture their real talent does not come without strings. The workplace of the next century is going to become a lot more like the professional sports team of the current century. That does not mean there will be no loyalty between the company and the employee. But it does mean that loyalty will have to be earned.

Vince Lombardi was tremendously loyal to the players on his old Green Bay Packers teams. But the players had to win Lombardi's loyalty by making a commitment to playing as well as they possibly could and then honoring that commitment. This meant that they showed up early for practice and worked terribly hard to get into condition, mindful of Lombardi's dictum that fatigue makes cowards of us all. They played with great intensity. If they didn't, they got no loyalty from Lombardi. What they got was traded.

Once they had Lombardi's loyalty and confidence, the coach gave the players a remarkable degree of autonomy. Bart Starr has recounted what happened as the final seconds ticked away in the famous Ice Bowl NFL championship game against Dallas in the 1960s. The ball was a yard from the Dallas goal. Starr called time out and trotted to the sideline. He told Lombardi he thought he could sneak it in behind guard Jerry Kramer.

Lombardi didn't argue, didn't equivocate. With the biggest play of the season coming up, he left the decision in Starr's hands. "Then do it," he said.

Kramer pushed Jethro Pugh of the Cowboys a foot or two back, Starr dove in, and everyone thought that Lombardi was a genius for calling the play. He was a genius, but not because he called that play. He was a genius for creating a situation in which players like Starr and Kramer could tap their real talents.

I hear occasionally from people who tell me that they can't get excited and passionate about their work because they think their company is going to mess things up—or mess them up—no matter how well they work.

I generally tell such people that most organizations aren't in the business of messing things up or failing to appreciate employees who are dedicated and committed. If they are, they don't last long. So if the complaining individual's company is an established one, I usually ask him to take another hard look at his own performance. Is he working as hard as Lombardi demanded the Green Bay Packers work?

Maybe what's happened is that this employee feels he proved his dedication and commitment when he started out. But new managers have come in, and he resents the fact that they don't seem impressed by the way he's performing. The hard fact is that there is going to be turnover in management in any large company. And you are going to have to prove yourself all over again to the new management. That's the way it is in sports. You prove yourself every day. And that's the way it increasingly will be in business. In a global marketplace, with global competition, it can't be any other way.

Maybe, though, the hard look just confirms that this is the anomalous company, the one that does mess up, the one that fails to appreciate its good employees, the one that deserves no loyalty. In that case, my advice is to get out. If you want to be committed and passionate about your work, you deserve a workplace that earns your loyalty by appreciating and making good use of your commitment and your passion. Find another job. Start your own business. But don't waste your life and your passion working for an organization that can't or won't appreciate it.

If you're a manager, on the other hand, once you have recruited someone with real talent, you must appreciate what that person can do for you, your organization, and himself.

You have to believe in him. You have to earn his loyalty. You have to give him a chance to shine.

When I was a freshman in high school, I had a basketball coach who had that kind of attitude. I remember an early season game that came down to the final minute all tied up. We got the ball and called time. The coach told me to run the clock down to a few seconds, drive to the basket, and take the final shot.

As it happened, I was double-teamed, I passed off to an unguarded teammate, and he shot the winning basket. I thought I'd done well. But afterward, the coach was furious with me.

Because he'd had faith in me, I was ready to listen to him. I asked him why he was upset, since we'd won the game.

"Because you're our best free throw shooter," he explained. "If you take the shot, you're likely to get fouled and make your free throws even if you miss the shot. And the guy you passed off to has the worst hands on the team. He might have mishandled the pass. And he's not a good free throw shooter. So when I tell you to take the shot, I want you to take the shot."

How could I not love the guy? From that moment on, I would have marched across Vermont barefoot in the snow if he'd asked me to.

That's the kind of loyalty a good manager inspires if he understands and nurtures real talent.

CHAPTER FOURTEEN

Writing Your Autobiography

I had a visit recently from a new client, a young man named Tom Scott. Tom's father is an excellent golfer and Tom grew up with a chance to take golf lessons and play often. But like a lot of us, he preferred other sports when he was in school— football, basketball, and lacrosse in his case. Then, in his twenties, he was too busy establishing a career to have much time for golf. It's only been in the last couple of years that he's had a chance to play seriously again. Now the game has hooked him, and he wants to see how good he can get.

We worked for a couple of days on getting Tom to be looser and freer on the golf course, the way he used to attack all sports when he was a kid. Tom showed me he has the chance to become a fine golfer. But what most impressed me was what he said about the nongolfing side of his life.

Tom had two experiences in his college years that shaped his attitude toward adulthood. The first came when he took a semester off from Brown University to attend a three-month National Outdoor Leadership School program in Wyoming. Tom and a group of similarly inexperienced outdoorsmen and outdoorswomen had to learn to survive in winter weather in the mountains. Frequently, the temperature dropped to ten below zero. The conditions forced the group members to find and develop resources within themselves, resources that perhaps they didn't know they had.

Tom appreciated the fact that within this group, status didn't depend on money, or clothes, or possessions. It depended on how hard people were willing to work to learn the skills they needed to get along and survive. He saw people come close to quitting, persevere, and eventually thrive. He saw them, in other words, acquire and develop real talent. The experience, he told me, taught him that "people can do anything if they don't get caught up in baloney."

Back at school, he found his classmates caught up in an entirely different spirit. As Tom saw it, they were all too eager to cut themselves a big slice of baloney. He remembers seeing one classmate diligently practicing his signature so it would look good on the cover letters he was sending with his résumé to Wall Street banking firms. Tom decided he did not want that kind of life. He decided to create a different life for himself.

He had a better idea of where he wanted to live than of how he was going to make a living. He loved Nantucket island, off the coast of Massachusetts. One summer, while he was at

Brown, he had worked as a taxi driver there. The next summer, he traded an old Volkswagen to his father for a twenty-two-foot Boston Whaler boat with an outboard motor. With the boat, he established a business called Nantucket Allserve. The staples of the business were coffee, muffins, and newspapers. Every morning, Tom would deliver them to the pleasure boats moored in Nantucket harbor. Then Tom did whatever odd jobs the boat owners had for him, from minor engine repairs to unclogging a vessel's septic system.

He liked it. He was working for himself. He was working hard, from early in the morning till late at night. He remembers thinking, "So this is what Dad meant when he talked about busting your butt to get ahead."

This was another lesson in real talent. He found that if he was doing something he loved, he loved to work.

After graduation, in 1989, Tom persuaded a friend named Tom First to go down to Nantucket with him and work in the Nantucket Allserve business. They did fine the first summer, but once the summer ended, they fell on hard times. They scratched for work wherever they could find it. They dug for scallops. They delivered fish.

And they started to experiment with making juice. Tom First had spent a summer in Spain and fallen in love with a local peach nectar called jugo de melocatón. Using a blender, he set about trying to duplicate the taste he remembered.

The two guys liked making juice, and they figured, correctly, that that juice would give them a new product they could sell to boat owners the following summer. They needed a name for their product. They decided to call it Nantucket Nectars.

They had definite ideas about quality. The American juice business generally adds high-fructose corn syrup to fruit juices because it's much easier to handle in the manufacturing process. The two Toms decided their product would use only cane sugar. They designed distinctive bottles. They developed interesting new flavors.

By the middle of the next summer, they had to find a soft drink factory to make enough juice to keep up with the demand. They were on their way.

The rest is not quite history. Tom and his partner have had ups and downs in the ensuing years. They've had juices turn green and juices explode on store shelves. They've had to teach themselves about pasteurization and microbe biology for their various fruit concoctions. They've taken on an investor who owns half the company. They got into the distribution business and lost a pile of money at it. They had to move their headquarters to Boston to keep track of trucks and warehouses.

They've gotten through the hard times by applying real talent, by being willing to do whatever it took to keep going. At one point, that meant taking on odd jobs like shampooing dogs. At another point, it meant making tough decisions like the one to move to Boston (though Tom still plans to return his office to Nantucket one day). It meant learning lessons from their mistakes in the distribution business and turning those lessons to their advantage when they contracted out that segment of the operation. "Our distributors love us because they know we understand their operations and their requirements," Tom told me.

Their business has grown dramatically. As Tom puts it, "We liked our juice. We liked selling it. Our entrepreneurial instinct took over." The company now has more than a hundred employees and in the last fiscal year recorded sales of more than $50 million.

~❦~

All of this stems, I believe, from the fact that Tom Scott found real talent within himself and decided he could accomplish anything he wanted to do. It shows what an individual with the right attitude is capable of.

Now that you've read this far, you have some questions to answer and some choices to make, much as Tom had choices to make when he left college and when his business nearly failed in its early years.

Are you going to do what you love, or learn to love what you do? Are you going to chase your dreams?

Do you want to be the best you can possibly be at what you do or do you, in your heart, want to settle for a safe mediocrity?

Are you going to listen to your highest aspirations, or are you going to listen to some "expert" who tells you you're not

213

talented enough? Are you going to try to have a Hall of Fame career, or are you going to give in to the peer pressure that wants you to be average?

Are you going to succumb to fear of failure, to doubt, and risk nothing, or are you going to free yourself of fear, laugh at it, and strive for excellence?

Are you going to believe in the power of your will and your mind and take responsibility for what you do with them? Or are you going to pretend that your destiny is out of your control?

Are you going to indulge in self-pity when you encounter the inevitable rejections and failures? Or are you going to learn what you can from your mistakes and move on?

Are you going to train yourself to think confidently, or are you going to succumb to the fiction that you can only be confident after you've succeeded?

Are you going to make and keep a commitment to put out your best effort every working day, or are you going to get complacent and slide by whenever you can?

If these sound like stark, dramatic choices, it's because they are. But these are the choices that will determine the course of your life.

If you think about it, you will realize that we are all on roughly the same footing when we start out. We're born to a mother. We have no control over who and when. Nor do we control, within certain limits, when we die. But we all control what happens in between. We control our lives. Some of us find strength within ourselves—in the mind, the heart, the gut, or the soul—that is infinitely more valuable than physical strength. Some of us don't. Some of us choose to do the hard things. Some of us don't.

In a very real sense, you are writing your autobiography every day of your life. You're choosing whether yours will be a life story that your grandchildren and great-grandchildren will pull from the shelf and marvel at because you made so much of the chances you had, or whether it will be a slender volume, devoid of drama and achievement, with a melancholy ending.

You have a chance to develop real talent, to develop the traits that will lead to success and happiness. Real talent will enable you to write a great autobiography—if you so choose.

Choose wisely.

Rotella's Rules

1. Real talent is something anyone can develop.

2. We are all underachievers. It's just a question of whether we get 40 percent out of the abilities we have or 90 percent.

3. In most of life's endeavors, characteristics like persistence and self-discipline are much more important than the kind of talent measured by standardized tests.

4. Success in high school has little or nothing to do with success in life.

5. If you think of yourself as able to do something, you probably will do it. If you think of yourself as incapable, you probably won't.

6. Every human being has the ability to choose how he thinks about himself and how he acts.

7. As George Burns put it, "You can either do what you

love or love what you do. I don't see where there's any other choice."

8. People who chase their dreams do what they love and they go for greatness.

9. A dream without a commitment is just a fantasy.

10. People with great dreams can achieve great things. People with small dreams can't.

11. When people with real talent approach any endeavor, they look for a method, a process, that will lead to success. Then they follow that process every day. They set themselves up to succeed.

12. Patience alone doesn't get you anywhere. You have to be patient while doing the right things.

13. A vision of what they can become is what enables some people to maintain and honor the commitments they make while others falter and give up. The ones who maintain their commitments are sustained by a vision of themselves as they would like to be. The ones who falter are those who rely on progress to sustain their motivation. When progress stops, so does their commitment.

14. People with real talent believe they can accomplish anything they set their minds to until proven otherwise. People with real talent have confidence.

15. Many people unwittingly use "realism" as a justification for thinking negatively and limiting themselves.

16. I don't often use the term "positive thinking." I like the

term "honest thinking," because that's what confidence really is.

17. I don't ask that you walk around all day telling yourself what a swell, capable person you are. All I ask is that you eliminate the negative thoughts.

18. People with real talent fail, just as do people without real talent. What sets them apart is the way they respond to failure.

19. Role models and mentors play an important part in the success of people with real talent. They can impart skills, either by example or by actively teaching us. More important, they can help us keep our commitments.

20. You will rarely, no matter what your field or where you work, find a role model who checks exactly the same boxes on the personnel form that you check. But you can almost always find someone who does a few things—perhaps no more than one or two—that you'd like to do.

21. People with real talent usually manage to surround themselves with people who support their quest to make the most of their talent, whether it be in golf or any other endeavor.

22. People with real talent compete primarily against themselves. Their quest is to see how good they can get.

23. People with real talent constantly find new ways to challenge themselves, new ways to invigorate themselves, especially when they reach middle age. They avoid burnout.

24. You can only coast in one direction.

25. In any endeavor, successful managers find that half their battle is won if they can identify and recruit people with real talent.

26. If you're a manager, once you have recruited someone with real talent, you must appreciate what that person can do for you, your organization, and himself. You have to believe in him. You have to give him a chance to shine.

ACKNOWLEDGMENTS

I am, as always, blessed with many people to thank. Many of the people mentioned in the pages of this book gave generously of their time and insights. I am grateful to them all.

I would like to single out for particular gratitude some people who, over the years, have given me opportunities to practice and sharpen my skills. In no particular order, they are: Linda Bunker of the University of Virginia; Nick Thomasetti, now president of Airbus Industrie; Pat Walsh at Merrill Lynch; Bob Collins at General Electric; Terry Holland, former basketball coach and now athletic director at the University; John Calipari, coach of the University of Massachusetts and the New Jersey Nets; Jim Larranaga, now coach of George Mason University's basketball team; Jim Lefebvre, former manager of the Seattle Mariners and the Chicago Cubs; Johnny Oates, Doug Melvin, and Dick Bosman of the Texas Rangers; and Doug Vaughn and Richard Ballard of the Pepsi Cola Company. I'm grateful to them all.

And, of course, I'm indebted to my editor, Dominick Anfuso, at Simon and Schuster, for his help with this book and the three that preceded it.

ABOUT THE AUTHORS

Dr. Bob Rotella is the nation's premier sports psychologist and performance enhancement consultant. His clients in professional golf include Tom Kite, Davis Love III, David Duval, Brad Faxon, Billy Mayfair, and many other tournament winners. He consults with baseball's Texas Rangers, Hendrick Motor Sports of the NASCAR circuit, and the New Jersey Nets of the NBA. In the business world, his clients include Merrill Lynch and Pepsico. For two decades, he was director of sports psychology at the University of Virginia. He lives with his wife, Darlene, and their daughter, Casey, in Charlottesville, Virginia.

Bob Cullen is a journalist and novelist. This is his fourth collaboration with Dr. Bob Rotella. He lives with his wife and children in Chevy Chase, Maryland.

Dr. Bob Rotella and Bob Cullen may be reached online at 71370.1620@compuserve.com.